INTERPRETING
PROJECTIVE
DRAWINGS

INTERPRETING PROJECTIVE DRAWINGS

A Self Psychological Approach

Marvin Leibowitz, Ph.D.

USA	Publishing Office:	BRUNNER/MAZEL *A member of the Taylor & Francis Group* 325 Chestnut Street Philadelphia, PA 19106 Tel: (215) 625-8900 Fax: (215) 625-2940
	Distribution Center:	BRUNNER/MAZEL *A member of the Taylor & Francis Group* 47 Runway Road, Suite G Levittown, PA 19057 Tel: (215) 269-0400 Fax: (215) 269-0363
UK		BRUNNER/MAZEL *A member of the Taylor & Francis Group* 1 Gunpowder Square London EC4A 3DE Tel: +44 171 583 0490 Fax: +44 171 583 0581

INTERPRETING PROJECTIVE DRAWINGS: A Self Psychological Approach

1 2 3 4 5 6 7 8 9 0

Printed by Edwards Brothers, Ann Arbor, MI. 1999.
Cover design by Claire O'Neill.

A CIP catalog record for this book is available from the British Library.
∞The paper in this publication meets the requirements of the ANSI Standard Z39.48-1984 (Permanence of Paper).

Library of Congress Cataloging-in-Publication Data
Leibowitz, Marvin.
    Interpreting projective drawings : a self psychological approach /
Marvin Leibowitz.
        p.   cm.
    Includes bibliographical references and index.
    ISBN 0-87630-933-3 (alk. paper)
    1. Projection (Psychology)   I. Title.
BF 175.5.P68L45 1999
155.2´84—dc21   99-12635
                                                                      CIP

0-87630-933-3

To Valerie,
who made it happen

CONTENTS

PREFACE

Projective drawings, e.g., the House-Tree-Person Test (H-T-P), Draw-A-Person (DAP), Human Figure Drawing (HFD), or Kinetic Family Drawings (K-F-D), are commonly included in diagnostic batteries, assessment procedures, and as a method to measure change resulting from psychotherapy. However, there is a great deal of negative evidence with regard to their reliability and validity. Why, then, are they so frequently used? To some degree, the answer seems to lie in the experience of the examiner wherein drawings often exert a compelling *pull* in reflecting something valid about the drawer. For example, a house that is drawn with no walkway, a tiny door, few or shuttered windows, and no smoke coming from the chimney, conveys a sense of barren isolation that is hard to dismiss.

The purpose of this book is to provide the student or clinician working with a set of drawings with an entry into the subjective world of the patient that may not be readily discernible from the patient's verbal presentation.

The subjective world may be conceptualized in terms of aspects of self-structure and self-in-the-world that may have a direct bearing on the foci for the ensuing psychotherapeutic endeavor, and later, upon retesting, as a means of assessing progress, regression, and new foci.

The current work attempts to provide a detailed step-by-step, theoretically based technique for elucidating personality characteristics. For the student learning the procedure or the practicing clinician utilizing it in order to assess a patient, this book offers a *user-friendly* method that guides the assessor in employing an empathic approach to obtain a first, global impression and then a comprehensive structural analysis—a feature-by-feature personality profile—accompanied by illustrations. The importance of the *chromatic* (color) dimension is amply demonstrated. In addition, this work identifies not only problematic areas but elaborates *optimal* or *positive* characteristics as well.

Psychoanalytic self psychology, introduced by Heinz Kohut, serves as the theoretical underpinning for this work. Kohut's emphasis on *self struc-ture* and the importance of the *selfobject experience* relates directly to the underlying basis for all projective testing—the representation of one's own characteristics, traits, and dynamics, and that of significant figures in one's life, in one's perceptions or productions. Furthermore, Kohut's focus on the process of *empathic immersion* into the world of the patient's *subjective experience* serves as a means of gaining access into the meanings conveyed by his or her artistic productions.

As Hammer (1958) pointed out, the use of case studies and the pre- and post-therapy analysis of Projective Drawings (PDs) are important tools in establishing their reliability and validity. A recent study by Robins et al. (1991) demonstrated the significant improvement of HFDs for seri-ously disturbed young adults during the course of intensive inpatient treat-ment. The current work presents more examples of the *subject as his own control* than anything found in the field. Each separate drawing, (HOUSE, TREE, PERSONS, ANIMAL), as well as an integrated case (all *10* draw-ings, achromatic and chromatic), is presented from the beginning phase of treatment to its one- (or more) year status.

Given the absence of a firmly established statistical or empirical basis for the interpretation of projective drawings, the effort made here to en-ter the subjective world of the drawer in order to provide a method of gaining a sense of what the person is telling us about him or herself, may provide the best way to utilize drawings, usefully and meaningfully, at the current state of our knowledge.

ACKNOWLEDGMENTS

This book probably would not have been launched without the impetus provided by Gene K. Nebel, Ph.D., a "psychologist's psychologist," whose passion for psychological testing was infectious and inspirational.

In one of its incarnations, the project was given support and assistance by Robert McGrath, Ph.D., Professor of Psychology at Fairleigh Dickinson University. I would also like to thank those of his (and other) students who served as research assistants. Earlier, my colleagues at the Mental Health Clinic of Passaic helped me to hone my ability to interpret projective drawings. I would like to thank them for their interest and support.

Tremendous gratitude and appreciation goes to Susan E. Alexander, Ph.D. whose support, encouragement, and advice propelled me toward publication. Her introduction tp the manuscript of Irving B. Weiner, Ph.D. and John E. Exner, Ph.D., whom I would like to thank for their gracious reviews, was invaluable.

I would also like to express my appreciation to David S. MacIsaac, Ph.D., mentor, colleague, and friend who introduced me to the work of Heinz Kohut and who has been a continuing source of enlightenment and focus with regard to my understanding of self psychology.

During the many years that the work was developed, many colleagues offered help and support. I would particularly like to acknowledge Peggy Corbisiero, Psy.D., Judith A. Koch, Ph.D., Marc I. Lipkus, Psy.D., and Stephen B. Safran, Ph.D. for their exceptional assistance.

Lansing Hays and Toby Wahl, Acquisition Editors at Brunner/Mazel deserve special thanks for their help as do Production Editor Catherine Van Sciver, and Production Manager, Ed Cilurso for his extensive help with preparing the color art.

To my many friends and relatives whose somewhat puzzled reaction as to why the damn thing wasn't finished yet were nevertheless unfailingly encouraging and proud, I would like to extend my thanks and appreciation. My dear friends, Bruce and Sherry Friedman, Joan and Sandy Gelb, and Charles and Jan Honig were particularly supportive as were my sisters, Iris Brooks and Maryellen Ernest, my mother-in-law, Vivian Carter, my sister and brother-in-law, Karen and Gerry Dreyfus, my children, David and Karen, and my step-daughters, Wendi, Debbi, and Marci (and their spouses and my wonderful grandchildren), also Gil and Yona Kollin, and Steven and Michelle Leibovitz. My parents, Sam and Frances Leibowitz, would have been proud. To my wife, Valerie, for her patience and loving kindness, to whom I dedicate this work, I give my undying love and gratitude.

And to the patients, whose drawings were included in the book, as well as the many patients (and others) who trustingly provided me with their productions, my everlasting thanks and appreciation. "I couldn't have done it without you."

1

Introduction

Projective Drawings (PDs), primarily that of the human figure, have been used to assess personality and/or intellectual functioning since the 1920s (Goodenough, 1926). Mostly utilized in evaluating childrens IQs, Goodenough found that her Draw-A-Man Test also yielded considerable personality data. Drawings were included in full assessment batteries and extended to adult assessments as well. Machover (1949), employing a psychoanalytic approach, brought forth the first comprehensive monograph which attempted to attribute meaning to the drawn human figure in terms of both content (symbolic meaning) and structural factors, e.g., line quality, size, and placement. Buck (1948), writing at about the same time as Machover, extended this approach to drawings of the house and tree as well as the person. Hammer (1958) elaborated on Buck's work, producing a broad, sweeping work which included contributions from leading researchers on topics including expressive (structural) aspects of PDs, child, adolescent, and adult drawings, the use of drawings in pre- and post-therapy analysis, symbolism in animal drawings, as well as other uses of PDs in clinical assessment and art therapy.

Hammer and Buck's work on the H-T-P spawned a number of handbooks and catalogues, which consolidated the existing research literature in attempting to attribute meanings to the various aspects of PDs (Bieliauskus, 1980; Buck, 1966, 1992; Jolles, 1971; Mitchell et al., 1993; Ogdon, 1967, 1981; Urban, 1963; Wenck, 1977).

Much of the research that sought to establish the reliability and validity of the interpretations advanced by the above writers was severely challenged by Swensen (1957, 1968). Other surveys, (primarily of human

1

figure drawings), have also failed to support their reliability and validity (Harris, 1963; Kahill, 1984; Klopfer & Taulbee, 1976; Suinn & Oskamp, 1969). This has led several writers to advocate abandoning the HFD (or DAP) as a "test" to be included in clinical batteries but only to be used, at best, as part of the interview process (Anastasi, 1982; Joiner et al., 1996; Joiner & Schmidt, 1997; Gresham, 1993; Kamphaus & Pleiss, 1993; Knoff, 1993; Motta et al., 1993).

On the other hand, positive research findings have been reported. Riethmiller and Handler (1997a, 1997b), in response to Joiner et al. (1996), believe that PDs have considerable usefulness if individual signs are not used out of context, artistic ability and amount of detail are factored in or controlled, discriminations are made within details, (e.g., do erasures lead to improvements?, are there different *types* of shading?), drawing attributes are used as predictors of other test results, and most importantly, the making of mechanistic judgments is avoided but raters are asked for judgments within meaningful, specific contexts. They point to studies by Kot et al. (1994) in which drawings differentiated homeless men, hospitalized psychotic men, and normals; Yama (1990), who found that impressionistic ratings of drawings predicted number of foster care placements; and Tharanger and Stark (1990), who differentiated patients' level of depression using global ratings obtained through experiential and impressionistic methods.

Other positive results using PDs include the ability of HFDs to differentiate adjudicated and nonadjudicated adolescents (Marsh et al., 1991); assess concrete and abstract thinking (Gustafson & Wachler, 1992); indicate impulsivity (Oas, 1985); evaluate anxiety (Sims et al., 1983); determine gender role identification (Farlyo & Paludi, 1985; Houston & Terwilliger, 1995); correlate with field dependence/independence (Witkin et al., 1962); differentiate incest survivors from normal controls (Waldman et al., 1994); and accurately reflect body image (Hayslip, et al., 1997). An impressive degree of empirical validation has been achieved by Koppitz (1968, 1984) and Naglieri et al. (1988, 1991), utilizing the HFD and DAP to assess the intellectual and emotional status of children.

Regardless of the controversy surrounding the research-supported reliability and validity of PDs, and their use, particularly with respect to children and families (Burns, 1982; Burns & Kaufman, 1970, 1972; DiLeo, 1970, 1973; Klepsch & Logie, 1982; Oster & Gould, 1987; Reznikoff & Reznikoff, 1956), which is founded primarily on clinical experience, has flourished, largely because of their compelling sense of authenticity. Burns (1987) extension of the kinetic dimension to the H-T-P and his inclusion of adult subjects is an especially interesting application of PDs.

The debate regarding the legitimacy of PDs has largely centered on the human figure, drawn in pencil by children. Extending empirical research to the employment of multiple drawings from the same subject, (e.g., house, tree, and animal), and the addition of the chromatic dimension, has never been attempted to my knowledge. A large scale empirical study employing both normal and pathological populations similar to that done for the Rorschach by Exner (1993) would unquestionably help to establish projective drawings as a reliable and valid test instrument. Although this kind of validation is lacking, the application of a *theoretical* framework by which drawings can be interpreted, opens up an alternative approach that can provide the clinician with much useful information.

Reviewing the literature we find a lack of a consistent, explicit, comprehensive connection of theory and drawing. Although Machover, Buck, and Hammer employed the concepts of classical psychoanalysis (Freudian drive theory) in both a *broad* sense, i.e., the general idea that the individual projects her wishes, conflicts, and defenses onto her drawings and a *narrow* sense, i.e., certain aspects of particular drawings have specific symbolic meaning, e.g., chimney as phallic symbol, there has not been a systematic linkage in which theoretical constructs or concepts are interwoven into the interpretation of selected drawings.

An exception to this may be found in the work of Gillespie (1994) whose study, *The Projective Use of Mother-and-Child Drawings*, integrates relational theory with the interpretation of a subject's drawings of the mother-child dyad. She states:

> As the various projective drawing techniques have developed over the last 30 years , it is clear that prognostic validation, rather than research confirmation of the interpretations, has been the source of their popularity and utility in clinical experience. Theory has been scarce and of little importance. (p. 9)

The psychoanalytic self psychology advanced by Kohut (1971, 1977, 1984) and his followers (Basch, 1980; Chessick, 1985; Rowe & MacIsaac, 1989; Wolf, 1988) appears to offer an excellent theoretical vehicle with which to underlie the interpretation of projective drawings. Here, what is "projected" by the drawer are aspects of the person's experience of his/her self-representation as well as representations of the experience provided by *selfobjects*, i.e., persons or things or situations in the environment that the individual utilizes on a relatively primitive or mature level, to shore up or sustain the *self*. The selfobject phenomenon refers both to the individual's *experience* with relation to the relative gratification of particular selfobject needs and to the *source* of that experience. For purposes of simplification, the term *selfobject* as used in subsequent chapters will refer to both. With reference to other assessment techniques (Rorschach, Thematic Apperception Test [TAT], Minnesota Multiphasic Personality Inventory [MMPI]), Sola and Snyder (1996) have recently employed a self psychological framework to provide a methodology of investigation and a set of principles that direct the focus of the assessor. They emphasize the primacy of the experience of the client, which the assessor uses as a basis for an empathic connection with the individual's organization or structure of his self and of the intersubjective field. This approach is entirely consistent with my understanding of the use of the theory of self psychology as it may be applied to the analysis of projective drawings.

Kohut believed that introspection was the only valid method by which a person could observe his own inner world and that *vicarious introspection*, i.e., empathy, enabled one to learn the inner world of another person. Introspection and empathy are the perceptual tools for the exploration of the world of the subjective. They relate to the individual's inner personal experience as opposed to referencing this material against outside *objective* standards. They are a means of observation, of gathering subjective data. In so stating, Kohut differentiated introspective data from extrospective data, i.e., that which is acquired from outside the subject by means other than introspection or empathy. Although the subjective world is not graspable by extrospection, Kohut was open to the possibility that the extrospective mode might assist the introspective method (Lee & Martin, 1991). In this direction, extrospective data such as case history material or other objective data such as personality tests may provide the psychological investigator, assessor, or therapist with valuable clues—a starting point—into the inner world of the patient. If the investigator adopts an empathic attitude toward the material, i.e., attempts to put himself into the shoe's of the person by means of what the material may represent to the person, rather than solely about the person by outside standards, then such expressions, e.g., drawings, of the person's inner state may serve as a source of material much as words spoken from the analytic couch. In fact, drawings may facilitate access to such material and, in situations in which verbal expression is difficult or impossible to acquire, actually provide the only source of such information.

In addition to the concept of the *selfobject*, the theoretical constructs advanced by Kohut that are salient to the present work include his definition of the self as being comprised of at least three sectors. One sector consists of the child's *exhibitionistic* and *grandiose* needs that have to be *mirrored* (i.e., reflected, recognized, and admired) by empathic selfobjects in order for optimal development to proceed. This process is often referred to as the child experiencing the "gleam in the mother's eye" and, as the self matures, leads to healthy self-esteem, ambition, and assertiveness. A second sector of the self consists of *idealizing* needs. The child requires a powerful selfobject to idealize and seek strength and soothing in times of distress. Optimally, this function is internalized as the capacity for self-soothing and the adoption of the values and ideals of the selfobject. Kohut added a third constituent of the self (1984) that was called *alterego* or *twinship* needs. This comprises the need for the child to experience him/herself as being like someone similar to oneself, i.e., the need for human kinship. Optimally, this matures into a self that develops the talents and skills that unfold from shared experience with an empathic selfobject.

Projective drawings can illuminate these aspects of the mature self. They can also reveal the manifestations of developmental deficits or deficiencies resulting from a lifetime of exposure to unempathic selfobjects that preclude the growth of a cohesive self. Insufficient mirroring, unavailability of idealized selfobjects, and inadequate human closeness result in the fragmentation of the self and subsequent cognitive, affective, and behavioral pathology.

It is anticipated that the investigator utilizing these concepts in the interpretation of PDs will avail him/herself of a thoroughgoing exploration of the work of Kohut and other expositors of self psychological theory.

Although the interpretive framework utilized in this work centers mainly on the self-selfobject matrix advanced by Kohut, elaborations of the theory of self psychology advanced by Stolorow et al. (1987, 1994) and Lichtenberg et al. (1989, 1992) inform the thinking which underlies the application of the theory to the analysis of projective drawings.

The former's concept of the *intersubjective field* is incorporated in the understanding that the interpretation of the subjective state revealed in the drawings is intimately interwoven with the subjective state of the assessor as he attempts to become immersed in and elucidate what is conveyed by the drawings and elicited within him.

Lichtenberg et al. define the self in terms of its capacity to organize experience and to initiate action. The latter is linked to the idea of motivation. Five subsystems are proposed that motivate the self: 1) the need for psychic regulation of physiological requirements, 2) the need for attachment-affiliation, 3) the need for exploration and assertion, 4) the need to react aversively through antagonism or withdrawal, and 5) the need for sensual enjoyment and sexual excitement. With the exception of (1), these motivational elements are identified and specified when revealed as behavioral or experiential manifestations of self-organization by the person in her drawings.

The interpretations offered in this work may also be conceptualized in terms of a broader *relational* approach in which aspects of self-experience and the drawer's experience of significant objects are the operative principles. The theoretical positions may encompass object relations, interpersonal, and existential theory (cf. Bacal & Newman, 1990).

With regard to the use of color in projective drawings, Hammer (1958) is mainly responsible for introducing the chromatic dimension. He emphasized that the use of crayons following the use of the pencil (achromatic dimension) permits the interpreter to gain access to somewhat different levels of personality. He maintained that chromatic projective drawings lay bare a *deeper* level of personality. Color is more closely associated with emotion; it is associated with childhood experience, and because it comes after the achromatic phase, may find the subject in a more vulnerable state. Hammer maintained that improvement from the *achromatic* to the *chromatic* drawings was a favorable prognostic sign while the reverse suggested greater pathology. Applying a "self" orientation, it may be hypothesized that the achromatic phase offers the subject an opportunity to represent one's self-state and one's selfobject world as they are experienced in the *here-and-now*, as the current, "real," intellectual, emotional, and interpersonal experience of life. On the other hand, the chromatic dimension appears to offer an opportunity to represent a level of experience that may or may not be removed from what the individual experiences as his functional reality. It affords a greater range of affective expression and permits access to a continuum of experience, ranging from an idealized, wished-for dimension, through a functional equivalence with the day-to-day reality orientation, to a level of fear and hopelessness.

The interpretations accompanying the use of color in this work mainly follow the writing of Luscher (1969), whose detailed analysis of the experiential components of the different colors for the individual, seems to correspond more closely to the self psychological orientation that informs the understanding of the subjective meanings of the drawings.

The drawings that will be analyzed in the following pages are those of a HOUSE, TREE, PERSON, PERSON OF THE OPPOSITE SEX, and ANIMAL. These were selected because each offers specific aspects of self and selfobject experience and all provide generic aspects of these experiences.

These drawings provide the psychologist with an opportunity to empathize with the experiential state of the drawer on different levels of assessment. On an impressionistic level, for example, does the HOUSE seem cold or cheerful? Does the ANIMAL seem ferocious or docile?

Each drawing can also be analyzed in detail with regard to characteristics related both to the self and to the provider of selfobject experiences. For example, the HOUSE may represent to the drawer a source of warmth, security, and support. It may encompass the significant figures associated with the home—typically family members—in terms of their accessibility, approachability, and stability. Correspondingly, it may represent what the person has internalized into her self-structure from her experience with this selfobject source and what is manifested in terms of the person's own sense of stability, security, approachability, etc.

In a similar fashion, the MALE and FEMALE drawings may represent to the drawer both a provider of selfobject needs as well as a self-representation. In the former case, the figure may manifest impressions and perceptions of a significant other, e.g., their aggressivity, passivity, and/or compulsivity. This may be particularly true for the drawing of the person of the opposite gender from the subject. With regard to the self, the drawings of the MALE and FEMALE figures may depict characteristics related to the drawer's own self-image and self-concept.

The TREE and ANIMAL drawings appear to pull more for characteristics related to the self than for those that might be attributed to a selfobject source. The TREE provides a comprehensive image of self-structure including interactional potentials, inner strength, and connection to internal processes. The ANIMAL illuminates primitive aspects of self-structure. Selfobject attributions may also be ascribed to aspects of both of these drawings; e.g., the setting for the TREE may represent the person's experience of his environment, the ANIMAL may refer to a significant person in the drawer's world of experience.

2

Using Projective Drawings in Practice–Impressionistic Analysis

Although projective drawings (PDs) can be used in any setting, for many purposes, (e.g., diagnosis, assessment, research, progress in therapy), and with any population, this work is targeted toward an adult population in a therapy setting, by a clinician with a knowledge of projective testing and the theory of self psychology.

Many adults will be somewhat resistant to the idea of providing drawings. This may be based on feelings of inexperience, inadequacy, or suspicion with regard to their use by the therapist. These objections can be countered by emphasizing the therapist's interest in extending his/her knowledge about the patient and not in assessing his artistic ability. The therapist can offer to share the findings with the patient. If it does not seem appropriate to take up therapy time, the patient can be given the opportunity to perform or complete the task at home (see Appendix A for Instructions by Examiner or Self).

Many therapists are reluctant to interfere with the therapeutic relationship or transference by engaging the patient in a directive manner and gaining information that the patient may experience as being out of her control. This may be less problematic for those therapists who emphasize an *empathic attunement* versus a *blank screen* orientation.

By presenting the opportunity to the patient for both therapist and patient to gain information that they can use in furthering the collaborative venture of psychotherapy, the perception of the therapist can be enhanced as a source of caring and knowledge (idealized transference) and as the two working together in a joint activity (twinship transference).

Of course, if a patient is very resistant or the therapist senses that introducing drawings would constitute an empathic break for that patient at
that time, the task can be postponed, either indefinitely or until a more
propitious time.

☐ Impressionistic Analysis

After completion of the drawings by the patient, the therapist should
react to each drawing, as a whole and/or to its parts, on an impressionistic level before engaging in a structural analysis that will focus on specific
interpretations associated with constituent components, e.g., the degree
of shading being related to the degree of anxiety.

As part of the impressionistic process, the therapist can physically take
the pose of the TREE, PERSONS, or ANIMAL (or make the facial expression of what the appearance of the HOUSE may be analogous to) in order
to kinesthetically empathize with what the patient may have been experiencing, consciously or unconsciously, as he or she drew.

Then, as the therapist looks at the drawing, he or she will get impressions that will range along a continuum from visceral and affective, e.g.,
"That house looks spooky," or "This person looks sweet," to more intellectual reactions, e.g., "This tree seems to be balanced." Impressions may
take the form of a metaphor, e.g., "This house looks like it's floating in
the air." Furthermore, the therapist should take into consideration her
personal reactions, e.g., "Do I like this house (tree, person, or animal)?"
"Would I like to live in this house?" "Would I like to meet this person?"
The therapist should record the adjectives, phrases, metaphors, or feelings that capture the "sense" of the drawing from any of these sources as
he vicariously experiences what the patient may have experienced as he
or she drew it. (See Appendix B for lists of adjectives for each figure that
may be helpful in evoking an empathic response. Be free to add adjectives or expressions that may not be included.)

The process of reacting to the overall feel of the drawing may hit the
observer with sudden impact or may develop slowly, with repeated
viewings. Thus, do not feel constrained to come up with an impression
on first viewing. Repeat the observational process and feel free to change
or modify first impressions. Often, permitting another observer to react
in a spontaneous fashion, may provide valuable insights.

The Impressionistic Analysis is not intended to constitute a full comprehensive method of mining PDs for what they can yield with regard to
understanding personality. For this, *both* the Impressionistic *and* Structural Analyses should be performed. The following examples of the former
are presented both to illustrate the process with case material and to pro-

vide the reader with an introduction to the empathic approach to working with projective data. These initial impressions are the *beginning* forays into the subjective world of the respondent. They can then be used to tie together into a meaningful whole, the separate interpretive elements gleaned through the structural analysis of the drawings.

☐ The HOUSE

The Case of Z. M.

Z. M., a 19-year-old student, was in treatment for depression related to a home situation with an oppressive father and a mother diagnosed as schizophrenic.

Figure 2.1, done at the beginning of treatment, shows his drawing of a HOUSE (chromatic drawings were not obtained). The impression is of a barren, cold, empty place—inaccessible, unapproachable, and closed off—floating off in space. He states that his family lives there; it's a "house of the first century . . . very poor." This may be seen as an expression of his experience of his selfobject milieu and as a reflection of his own impoverished sense of self.

FIGURE 2.1

Figure 2.2 was done after one year of treatment. This HOUSE and its setting give a feeling of being alive, accessible, and approachable. There is a feeling of warmth. This could reflect his experience of the treatment environment as a source of needed selfobject recognition. However, if the facade is seen as a face with the windows as eyes and the door as a mouth, there is a feeling of sadness. Also, there is a sense of instability and a lack of groundedness. These aspects point to insufficiencies in self-structure.

FIGURE 2.2

FIGURE 2.3

Figure 2.3 was done after two years of treatment. This HOUSE is impressive with its size, sturdiness, dimensionality, and presence. As a reflection of self-structure, we have a sense of someone whose inner cohesion, integrated capacity for grandiose exhibitionism, and self-esteem have undergone radical improvement.

The Case of G. G.

G. G., a 37-year-old, married, medical research scientist, reported a history of depressive episodes. He had been in therapy several times and, although not currently depressed, was re-entering therapy because "it was time to clear up unfinished business." He felt dependent and full of self-doubt. He described his father as an alcoholic, violent and confrontational; his mother was detached and ungiving.

Looking at the achromatic (pencil) HOUSE (Figure 2.4), this observer gets mixed feelings. I do not particularly like it or dislike it. It seems bland, somewhat cold but not forbidding. It looks approachable but set back, accessible but somewhat guarded.

Turning to the chromatic (crayon) HOUSE (Color Plate 1), we find essentially the same drawing but the feel of the drawing for this examiner is freer, looser, and less precise. There is less of a measured rigid feel.

What I take away from this level of analysis is a sense of a man who

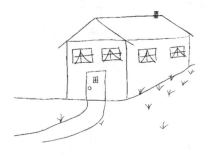

FIGURE 2.4

takes his responsibility to his family very seriously but needs to have the affective dimension (color) tapped in order to become less rigid and more human. It is interesting to note that in answer to the questions: "Who lives in this house?" and "What kind of feeling does it give you?", he responds: 1) "A family, husband and wife and three children and pet dog and cat," and 2) "Sturdy, secure, lively, warm"—

to the *pencil* drawing; and then, to the *crayon* drawing: 1) "Large" family—spouses (husband and wife) and four children and maternal grandmother and many pets (dogs, cats, hamsters, and fish)," and 2) "Feelings—chaotic but warm on the inside."

Thus, at the beginning of therapy, we speculate that a possibly significant issue for G. G. will be a need to reconcile a tendency to become

FIGURE 2.5

somewhat rigid or constricted when functioning in the world of responsibility with a wish for a freer, fuller, more affectively rich life experience.

What do we find after one year of therapy? The pencil HOUSE (Figure 2.5) appears to be alive, spilling over with stuff. The rigid quality is gone.

This is even more pronounced in the color drawing (Color Plate 2). The questions are now answered: "1) A family 2) Big, solid, open, and warm" (*pencil* drawing);"1) A family 2) "Great feeling from house—comfortable, lots of things to do inside and outside. Aroma of supper on the stove, lots of kids inside." (*crayon* drawing).

We can speculate that G. G.'s self-structure permits more flexibility and openness and greater expansiveness and warmth with regard to the selfobject milieu of the home.

☐ The TREE

The Case of X. N.

Here we have the TREE drawings of X. N., a 45-year-old divorced man who entered therapy because of increased drinking, pressure at work and from his exwife, and loss of self-esteem when his girlfriend dropped him. He felt angry, anxious, and depressed. After six weeks of weekly sessions he began to be seen on a biweekly basis. Approximately nine weeks after beginning therapy, projective drawings were obtained.

The achromatic TREE (Figure 2.6)

FIGURE 2.6

FIGURE 2.7

appears to be alive, realistic, and mature but with a sense of reaching out without the inner structure or development to fulfill the outreach. Also, the trunk has a careless, unfinished look and its connection to the ground is not solid. The patient describes it as "100 years old, alive, in the spring."

The chromatic TREE (Color Plate 3) appears somewhat vibrant and "Christmasy" at first glance. However, it is rootless and seems to be floating with no grounding. The patient describes it as "Very young— less than a year. It's dead. It's Christmas (winter), sitting in the fire house lot."

Thus, near the beginning of therapy, the achromatic TREE drawing, as a reflection of self-concept in the day-to-day world, gives a mixed feeling of striving and hope but with a sense of inner insufficiency. On the affective (chromatic) level, again the picture is mixed. The colors are vivid, giving a sense of aliveness, but there is a feeling of inner emptiness and rootlessness. The overwhelming sense of depressed loneliness is reflected in the verbal description.

X. N. was again administered PDs after approximately four years of biweekly therapy. The achromatic TREE (Figure 2.7) seems to leap out into the environment. The branches seem angry, busy, and fluid. The page (i.e., the environment) barely contains it. At the same time, it is solidly rooted in the ground. This TREE is described by the patient as "40, alive, in the early summer."

Given the opportunity for affective expression, the color drawing (Color Plate 4), has more of a feeling of fluidly reaching out into the environment. The slimness of the trunk suggests an imbalance between striving and a sense of capacity to sustain it; but the solidity of the base of the TREE gives a feeling of strength. Its description is identical to the achromatic TREE.

Contrasting the two sets of drawings gives a sense of how much more this person is able to express his grandiose exhibitionistic strivings within the context of a solid, integrated self-structure.

It should be noted that at the time of the second PDs, X. N. was overtly angry about his working conditions on the one hand, but extremely happy about his new marriage on the other.

☐ The PERSONS

The Case of N. T.

N. T., a 28-year-old woman, was a struggling actress when she entered therapy. Recently divorced, she felt unloved and unlovable. Her father had left the family when she was very young; her mother never remarried and had devoted herself to N. T.

Figures 2.8 and 2.9, N. T.'s first achromatic drawings of a MALE and FEMALE, look empty, ill-formed, inadequate, bland, and simple. It is as if she is saying, "I'm not worth the effort to make an effort." (Chromatic drawings were not obtained.)

The MALE is described as being 12-years-old, "in a playful mood, not too serious minded, just looking for something to do, not worthwhile, and more for fun. He's holding firmly to the ground and poised—ready to go into something physical."

The FEMALE is 17. She has "a vapid look, kind of dumb, oblivious, and pretty content. She doesn't look like she's on the brink of doing anything, sort of sitting around."

It appears that N. T. has consciously idealized the male role as freer, stronger, and more active. This is in contrast to a denigrated view of the female role—by extension, her own self-image.

One year later, after weekly therapy sessions, quite a different picture emerges. Figure 2.10, the MALE, looks frighteningly aggressive, menacing, leering, crazy, and dangerous. Figure 2.11, the FEMALE, nearly jumps off the page with hostility.

The MALE is now described as being

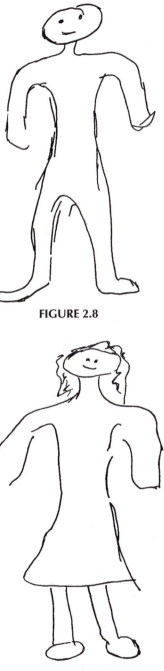

FIGURE 2.8

FIGURE 2.9

FIGURE 2.10

FIGURE 2.11

in his early 20's. Her description does not convey the fearfulness of the visual impression. She states that "He is a very physical person, doing physical labor. He looks poised and ready to do something. He doesn't feel anything. Not too bright. Just lives."

The FEMALE is 30–35 years old. "Her mouth is open. She's talking a lot. Telling all about herself to someone who doesn't care that much. Talks to stop feeling. No time to think about what she's feeling."

As before, the male role is more valued than the female. Therapy seems to have unleashed the underlying rage that results from experiencing an absence of empathic attunement from a source of self-object gratification. This may also be taken as a reflection of her experience in the transference relationship with the therapist.

One year later, the FEMALE (Figure 2.12) is now drawn first. There is a sketchy, ill-formed quality but the figure appears to be quite bulky with powerful shoulders and arms. The expression on the face is rather sweet. Adopting the stance of the figure, with the palms turned out, one gets the feeling, "Well, how about it world? What do you have in store for me?" She describes the figure as "young, innocuous, with her arms out, just sort of greeting. Nothing special." It is as if she is inchoate—no longer angry but with a growing sense of power and an undefined, hopeful quality.

The MALE (Figure 2.13) looks bland with mitten-like hands as opposed to the differentiated fingers of the female. He can stand on his own two feet and is still described as very physical. N. T. states, "He's built like the girl I drew—in his case, brawny."

These figures may reveal a shift in the transference to the patient's experience of being mirrored for her own strength, thus experiencing herself as having greater physical ability—closer to the idealized male role.

After approximately three and one-half more years of therapy the final set of drawings was obtained from N. T. Adjectives which seem to fit Figure 2.14, the FEMALE, include active, alert, approachable, assertive, calm, capable, confident, feminine, free, friendly, happy, healthy, intelligent, normal, open, peaceful, pleasant, quiet, realistic, sane, solid, strong, warm, and young (see Appendix B). The figure is described as "in her 30's, taking a walk, and feeling fine."

The MALE figure (Figure 2.15), appears to have a somewhat anxious, apprehensive expression. The fingers of the right hand are poorly articulated and his clothing is less differentiated than the female's. He is described as "in his 30's, almost running, and satisfied."

Compared to the previous drawings, both figures are more mature sexually and more defined as human beings. The FEMALE figure appears to have some conflict in the sexual area but the overall progression of N. T.s drawings provides a compelling sense of an improved self-structure and a sense of confident well-being.

At the time, N. T. had made significant gains in her profession and was

FIGURE 2.12

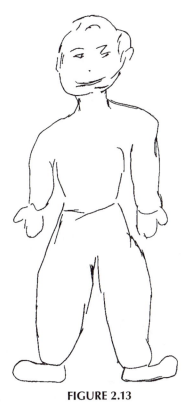

FIGURE 2.13

FIGURE 2.14

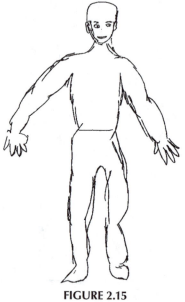

FIGURE 2.15

involved in a mostly stable, though problematic, relationship with a male.

The Case of E. K.

E. K., a 25-year-old newly married man, entered couples therapy with his wife. She complained that he was lazy and inconsiderate; their sex life was virtually nil. E. K., in his second year of business school (having failed to get into medical school), was obese, passive-aggressive, and depressive. The middle child and only son of a successful physician father and homemaker mother, he was totally dependent financially on his parents. He experienced his father as aloof and disapproving and his mother as favoring his sisters.

The couple was seen on a weekly basis for approximately nine months. Couples therapy ended when E. K.'s wife separated from him. He continued in individual weekly treatment.

Figures 2.16 and 2.17 were obtained when E. K. began individual therapy. Impressionistically, both the MALE and FEMALE can be seen as the quintessential "sad sacks." Only negative adjectives, such as anxious, fearful, depressed, dull, inadequate, lonely, meek, sad, submissive, withdrawn, weak, seem to apply to either figure.

The MALE is described by E. K. as "25, not thinking much, looking sad and a little surprised—he heard bad news. He's just looking."

The FEMALE is "25, no expression on her face at all. Just standing there." He adds, "I don't like the drawing. The waist is too thin."

Seen either as self-representations or as possible sources of selfobject support, E. K.s drawings seem like the most lost of "poor souls."

Approximately one year later, E. K.'s drawings of a MALE and FEMALE (Figures 2.18 and 2.19), show no improvement. The MALE figure is even more passive and enervated. He is described as "25, just sitting at his desk. Seems a little bewildered and afraid, not of anything in particular."

The FEMALE is "25, not doing anything. Just standing there. Not thinking or feeling."

Only after one more year of therapy do the drawings evoke a positive response. The achromatic MALE (Figure 2.20) looks alive, alert, approachable, friendly, happy, masculine, pleasant, and warm. Although seated, he does not seem passive. He is described as "Sitting cross-legged. He's pretty pleased, my age (27), looking out, with a pleasant anticipation on his face."

FIGURE 2.16

FIGURE 2.17

For the first time chromatic drawings were obtained. The MALE figure (Color Plate 5) impresses with its attempt to be a realistic self-portrait. (The patient looked somewhat like this figure.) If one adopts the pose, the hands feel as if they are guarding the genitals. The figure seems top-heavy, as if the leg area is not quite capable of supporting the head and chest. One is drawn to the heavily emphasized ears, arms and hands, and feet. "Can I make it if I stand on my own two feet?", the figure may be implying.

The achromatic FEMALE (Figure 2.21) has a pleasant, anticipatory look. She is full-chested but where is her lower body? She is "25, not doing very much. I don't know what she's thinking. She's just there." There is now a more benign, but, on a day-to-day level, still clueless sense of the female selfobject.

FIGURE 2.18

FIGURE 2.19

The chromatic FEMALE (Color Plate 6) is the most put-together figure so far. She impresses with her size, proportionality, and the evenness of the color distribution. She appears to be attractive, alert, capable-looking. She is described as "25, standing and waiting, and looking for somebody. She feels anxious." E. K. adds, "Her face looked like a skull (death) before I gave it color."

So after several years of treatment, although still anxious and uncertain, E. K.'s drawings indicate a growing readiness to tackle the world. With regard to the female selfobject, he seems to require the opportunity for affective expression (color) to go beyond his fear and to bring his feelings to life.

Finally, after approximately six years of therapy, Figures 2.22 and 2.23 were obtained. The achromatic MALE appears to be a realistic portrayal of an alert, well-balanced young man. The reinforced fingers are the only jarring note. He is described as "25, just standing there and not doing or thinking anything. Looks a little surprised." Experiencing himself in the "real" world, E. K. conveys a mostly solid, but still uncertain, sense of his ability to engage the world.

The achromatic FEMALE looks somewhat forbidding. Assuming the stance of this figure, one feels a loss of balance or a pulling-back. In his description of her, the patient states, "She's 25 and wondering how her face got to look like that. (I attempt to draw attractive women.) She's looking for a man, waiting for a man. Apprehensive, uncertain, wondering whether he'll come." Experiencing the female selfobject in the "real" world, E. K. seems to feel readier to approach but still unready and insufficient to achieve the recognition he longs for.

Color Plate 7 (chromatic MALE) and Color Plate 8 (chromatic FEMALE) seem to represent the most complete expression of the progress in self-development and selfobject relatedness that E. K. made in the course of treatment.

The MALE is an extremely accurate self-representation. E. K. had lost over 60 pounds in the course of leaving a successful career

FIGURE 2.20

start as an accountant, going back to college for pre-med courses, and being accepted in medical school. This figure looks out at the world with the "clear, cool look" of a mature young man who can stand on his own two feet. He is wearing a "power suit and tie," but his legs still look a little uncertain in terms of proving adequate support. He describes the figure as "25, waiting for something to happen. I don't know what he's thinking. He's anxious."

The crayon FEMALE appears pretty, "mod," but swaying backward somewhat. Her expression is a bit sad and her hand is an obvious source of unsettled feeling. She is "25 and looks like she's crying. Cut her hand. It hurts."

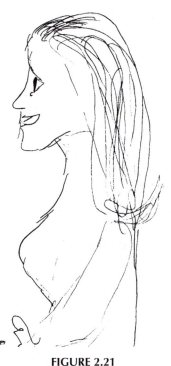

Here, the opportunity for affective expression elicits a softening of E. K.s perception of the female selfobject. "How much is she able to give me?", he seems to be asking. "Will there be pain in the giving?" These questions may be a reflection of the experiences with several women that E. K. had had after his divorce, relationships that achieved a complexity, both positive and negative, that were nowhere in evidence with his exwife.

Thus, it appears that E. K.'s figure drawings provide a reflection of the development of his strengthened self-structure and selfobject relatedness over the course of his psychotherapy. Com-

FIGURE 2.21

FIGURE 2.22   **FIGURE 2.23**

paring the two "sad sacks" at the beginning with the differentiated "human beings" at the conclusion, attests to the ability of the individual to reveal, through art, the capacity for change and growth.

☐ The ANIMAL

The Case of B. M.

B. M., a 23-year-old security guard, presented symptoms of a thought disorder. Orphaned at an early age, he was raised by his grandmother who had recently died. He had done poorly in school, had few friends and no sexual experience. He was referred because female coworkers found his manner and attempts to engage them somewhat threatening. A huge man, his insight and judgment were very poor but he had no history of acting-out.

Figure 2.24, drawn at the beginning of therapy, depicts his achromatic ANIMAL, a dog. The body and stance evoke a sense of strength and hypervigilant alertness. I immediately notice, however, that the upper part of the head is considerably

FIGURE 2.24

smaller than the mouth area. Within the mouth, the tongue has a decidedly phallic look. Impression: B. M. talks "dirty" and does not have the mental capacity to monitor or control himself—just what got him into trouble on the job.

The crayon ANIMAL, (Color Plate 9) is of a 100-year-old bat, using only black. The initial impression is frightening and menacing, until one looks more closely at the face which looks to me like that of a harmless baby.

These PDs seem to crystallize B. M.'s self-structure and self-in-the-world. Wanting desperately to be noticed, he attempts to utilize his size and strength to gain approval, but lacks the capacity to understand how distorted and inappropriate his attempts to communicate are. Having lost the selfobject support of his grandmother, disintegration anxiety results in a surge of sexual impulses.

On an affective level, his fear and dysphoria evoke a compensatory wish to frighten others but his sense of helplessness, his tendency to take flight rather than attack, predominate.

After a year in therapy, during which time he responded to the self-strengthening effects of an idealized selfobject transference, he produced Figure 2.25, an achromatic horse, and Color Plate 10, a chromatic dog.

The horse appears strong with a benign, even "goofy," expression. The connotation is of a potentially helpful and harmless animal.

The crayon animal is nicely balanced and gives a sense of moving and climbing (although its positioning in relation to the steps defies gravity). Emphasis is seen around the mouth—to keep it

FIGURE 2.25

shut! More warmth is seen in the addition of the brown color and in B. M.'s personalizing it as "my dog, Pete."

In summary, these drawings appear to demonstrate that therapy enabled this patient to experience a diminution of fear with the resultant channelizing of his grandiose-exhibitionistic needs into more appropriate channels.

3

CHAPTER

Using Projective Drawings in Practice–Structural Analysis– General Factors

While the Impressionistic Analysis is capable of affording the examiner a quick penetration into what PDs reveal about the self-state of the drawer, PDs can be analyzed in detail with regard to the *structural* aspects of drawings, e.g., line quality and shading, size, placement, color interpretation, as these relate to the various features of each of the drawings, e.g., for the HOUSE: the door, windows, walkway, etc., as well as to the drawing as a whole.

This analysis may provide a fuller, more comprehensive picture of the individual's self-structure and/or the way he experiences his selfobject world.

The structural aspects of drawings, or the way in which the individual executes the task, may be more meaningful than the actual content of the drawing. These aspects diffuse, to some extent, the argument regarding artistic ability negating the interpretation of PDs, i.e., the greater the ability, the "healthier" the drawings will appear.

When the examiner focuses on, for example, which features are drawn with heavier or lighter lines, what is the relative size of the features, and which colors are used to depict them, the idiosyncratic nature of the drawer's personality, regardless of drawing skill, begins to emerge. Structural aspects, e.g., the reinforcement of a door or windows, the disparity in size between the arms of a person, differential detailing, the placement of the TREE in a corner of the page, that leap out at the examiner, that engage her sensibility as she immerses herself in the drawing, provide the keys to the drawer's subjective experience.

☐ Interpretation of Structural Characteristics as Related to Whole Drawings

There is some basic agreement with regard to the meaning of structural aspects of PDs in the literature but no established body of empirical evidence to support these attributions.

If one applies the approach of self psychology, however, the interpreter of projective drawings can begin to penetrate the differential experience of the drawer during the process of drawing, and thus gain insight into his subjective state in relation to what is included, omitted, emphasized, etc.

Line Quality and Shading

Lines or outlines drawn to depict the different figures will vary on a continuum from faint or light through moderate to heavy or dark (or reinforced). Lines may also be drawn in a sketchy manner. This may be: a) "weak-sketchy"–weak, broken, or feathery rather than as a firm, solid line; or b) "firm-sketchy"–drawn with firm, short strokes in an "artistic" manner that promotes the perception of a solid line.

Lines may also be drawn in a tremulous manner, i.e., drawn in a wavy or jerky way that suggests tremor. Other aspects of how lines are drawn include being erased and redrawn (pencil only), drawnover, i.e., new lines inexactly superimposed on existing lines as opposed to heavily reinforcing a given line, or scribbled, i.e, drawn in a circular, repetitive, or haphazard manner. These variations also apply to shaded areas, i.e., areas in each of the figures that are filled in with pencil or crayon.

It is commonly held that these variations in line quality and shading are related to anxiety. Adopting an empathic position vis-a-vis the drawings, i.e., putting oneself into the position of the drawer, enables the examiner to go beyond the generic concept, "anxiety," and gain a sense of what the drawer experienced as she attempted to represent on paper her conceptual image, which will be suffused with both affective and cognitive associations attached to that concept.

a) Moderate and/or firm-sketchy line quality or shading. Moderate pencil or crayon pressure evoke a feeling of steadiness, of being unruffled, unhurried, and unpressured. It may be considered as an *optimal* expression of the drawer's affective expression vis-a-vis what the drawing represents.

Firm-sketchy line quality or shading evoke a feeling of involvement, of nuance that adds the dimension of *sensitivity* to the optimal expression.

b) Heavy or reinforced line quality or shading elicit a sense of intensity, pressure, force, strain—in short, *tension*.

c) Faint and/or weak-sketchy line quality or shading evoke a feeling of hesitancy, doubtfulness, indecision—in short, *uncertainty*.

d) Erased and redrawn pencil lines evoke a sense of *self-criticality*. The manner in which the lines are redrawn indicate the affect which accompanies the self-doubting.

e) Drawn over and/or scribbled line quality or shading elicit a hurried, impatient, and careless feel but with an underlying quality of felt-inadequacy that may be considered to be *avoidant anxiety*.

f) Tremulous line quality does not readily lend itself to empathic resonance. It appears to be outside the realm of optimal or dysphoric affect described above. It has been associated with the possibility of *neurological disturbance* and will be considered as such here.

Size

The size of the object or feature depicted may vary on a continuum from very large (huge) to above average (large) to average (moderate) to below average (small) to very small (tiny), or a feature may be omitted altogether. There are no recorded normative standards in the literature. Instead, the reference for whole objects in this study is the 8½" x 11" page and for separate features within the whole—the size of the object itself. Again, the judgment regarding size is based on the subjective sense of the examiner as he empathically places himself within the experience of the drawer.

Focusing on the subjective quality of variations in size in experiential terms, whole object size would appear to relate to the drawer's sense of adequacy, a readiness to position oneself in the world, and to permit oneself to be seen. This can apply to feelings about the self or significant selfobject.

a) Average or moderate size within the context of the size of the page would appear to indicate an *optimal* sense of adequacy—self and/or selfobject—in Kohutian terms, the depiction of a self with an appropriate level of grandiose/exhibitionism, or a selfobject with a similar self-structure or one who is capable of recognizing those needs.

b) Very large (huge) size elicits a feeling of excessive activity, of over-extending one's effort in order to be seen. If the figure runs over the page, the sense is of the drawer's feeling constricted or confined by her environment. It would suggest difficulty in the area of felt-adequacy with an excessive need for mirroring with *overcompensatory grandiose or exhibitionistic* behavior. If the object depicted is clearly identified as a selfobject, very large size may indicate an overcompensatory need in the area of idealization.

c) **Large or above average** size elicits a sense of willingness to make more than a *moderate effort* to achieve the gratification of mirroring or idealization needs.

d) **Small or below average** size elicits a sense of the drawer restricting his effort, of withdrawing because of a feeling of lessened capacity or *adequacy*. It may refer to the experience of a lesser availability of selfobject gratification of mirroring or idealization needs.

e) **Very small (tiny)** size evokes a sense of minimal effort—of *severe restriction* and *withdrawal*—into a world of isolation and depression. This may represent either a depleted self or a miniscule sense of selfobject gratification.

The amplified interpretations with regard to the size of separate features of the whole objects will be discussed and exemplified in future sections.

Placement

With regard to where on the page the subject chooses to place the object, the different possibilities—center, sides, corners, top or bottom—can be thought to relate to her subjective sense of how she *orients* herself in the environment.

a) **Center placement**. This conveys a feeling of *security, confidence, presence, and immediacy*—a capacity to relate in a here-and-now fashion. The actual placement should be somewhat off-center, i.e., slightly to the left or right of the vertical midline and slightly above or below the horizontal midline. *Exact* center placement evokes a feeling of *rigidity*, of needing to have everything exactly balanced in order to feel secure.

b) **Left placement**. Where the whole object is totally or almost totally placed to the *left* of the vertical midline, the sense is of movement toward an earlier position, to need a sense of what one may have previously experienced in the *past* in order to achieve a self-soothing affective state or to depict a selfobject experience which provides that kind of support.

c) **Right placement**. Where the whole object is totally or almost totally placed to the *right* of the vertical midline, the sense is of movement toward a *future* position, wherein the self or selfobject experience is pushed ahead, thought or imagined about, rather than dealt with forthrightly as in center placement.

d) Top placement. Where the whole object is totally or almost totally placed *above* the horizontal midline, the feeling is of evading here-and-now experience by "being in the clouds," i.e., utilizing excessive fantasy, either in relation to self-experience or to the experience of the selfobject. Also, one can vicariously attune to a sense of "rising above" the mundane, possibly accompanied by euphoric affect.

e) Bottom placement. Where the whole object is totally or almost totally placed *below* the horizontal midline, a sense of staying "low to the ground," of limiting one's thinking or affective state in a *concrete*, possibly *dysphoric* way may be vicariously evoked.

f) Corner placement. Where the whole object is totally or almost totally confined to a corner area no larger than one-half the length and one-half the width of the page, the subjective feeling is of *withdrawing* from here-and-now participation, of being fearful and lacking confidence.

> The *upper left corner* may emphasize *regressive fantasy*.
> The *upper right corner* may emphasize *future-oriented fantasy*.
> The *lower left corner* may emphasize *depressiveness related to the past*.
> The *lower right corner* may emphasize *hopelessness related to the future*.

The amplified interpretations with regard to the placement of separate features of the whole objects will be discussed and exemplified in future sections.

Color

Chromatic drawings are done using from one to eight crayons with no use of pencil whatsoever. The colors used are: BLUE, GREEN, RED, YELLOW, PURPLE, ORANGE, BROWN, and BLACK. As discussed earlier, the opportunity to draw in color opens up for the drawer a way to express a wider range of subjective experience than the use of pencil alone. What colors one picks to use, how extensively or selectively they are used, and with what aspect of line quality and shading are all structural aspects that can yield valuable clues concerning the capacity for *affective expression* of the drawer.

With regard to the whole object, if only one color is used, (or one color plus black), the subjective sense that is evoked is one of limited affective involvement vis-a-vis what the object represents—a feeling of constriction. Depending on the object depicted, using more than *four or five* colors evokes a feeling of unbridled affective involvement—of *lability*. The use of between *two and four or five* colors engenders a sense of affective *freedom and flexibility*.

The *manner* in which the crayons are used is also significant. If a crayon is used for the *outline* of the object mainly, with little or no inner shading, the vicarious experience elicited is one of *peripheral* involvement, a *holding back* of affect, a *reluctant*, or possibly *oppositional*, reaction to revealing more of one's inner affective state.

The different dimensions of line quality or shading, e.g., moderate, heavy, or light pressure, drawn-over lines, etc., add the respective affective qualities described previously, e.g., sensitivity, tension, uncertainty, etc., to the interpretation of the chromatic phase.

With regard to the subjective meanings attributed to the eight colors used, as stated above, Luscher's (1969) analysis of these colors provides the basis for understanding what the drawer may be experiencing as he/she engages in utilizing them in the drawing. The following summarizes these experiential qualities for each color.

BLUE. This color evokes a sense of *calmness, peace, and tranquility*. Its association with the sky or the sea adds to this interpretation. BLUE also engenders a sense of *contentment*. It conveys a feeling of *depth* rather than superficiality. If used extensively or inappropriately, it may relate to an excessive wish for a calm and orderly environment where relationships are placid and free from contention. This may also reflect a tendency to be easily hurt.

GREEN. This color evokes a sense of *aliveness and expansiveness*. It is associated with things that grow and with money. As such there appears to be a connection to what Luscher calls the "elasticity of will," i.e., the qualities of *self-preservation, persistence, self-assertion, obstinacy, and self-esteem*. If used extensively or inappropriately, GREEN may indicate a wish to increase certainty in one's own value either by self-assertiveness, holding onto an idealized image of oneself (or selfobject), or by wanting others to acknowledge or defer to one. It may reflect excessive grandiose-exhibitionistic strivings.

RED. This color evokes a sense of *excitement and desire*. It gives a feeling of *action*, even *impulsivity*. RED has a visceral quality (blood, the heart) that can be associated with *aggression* and/or *sexuality*. Its connotation is towards *competition, achievement, and success*. Used extensively or inappropriately, RED suggests an excessive wish for one's own activities to bring one intensity of experience and fullness of living.

YELLOW. This color conveys a feeling of *aspiration and relaxation*. Its association with the sun relates to feelings of *expectancy* (looking forward) and *exhilaration*. There is a sense of *spontaneity* with the use of YELLOW. If used extensively or inappropriately, it may relate to the excessive desire for release from burdens or restrictions and the hope or expectation of greater happiness.

PURPLE. This color, being a mixture of RED and BLUE, combines both a sense of the *impulsivity* of the former with the *gentleness* of the latter. The drawer may desire to be noticed and approved of as *special, unusual, and unique*. There is an element of *irresponsibility* and *immaturity* implied in its use. Extensive or inappropriate use may relate to the excessive wish to achieve a "magical" relationship, a wish to beglamor oneself, and, at the same time, charm and delight others. PURPLE's association to "royalty" may add the dimension of a wish for power over others or a feeling of entitlement.

ORANGE. Luscher does not discuss this color. As a mixture of YELLOW and RED, it may evoke contradictory feelings, i.e., the *relaxation and hope* of the former and the *action* and *excitement* of the latter. As such, it may relate to feelings of *ambivalence*. If used extensively or inappropriately, ORANGE may indicate excessive indecisiveness.

BROWN. This color suggests an association with the earth. As such, it conveys a sense of *rootedness* and a need for *security*. Luscher relates BROWN to sensation as it applies to the bodily senses, i.e., a need for *physical relaxation and ease*. This may also apply to a need for *interpersonal ease* and *security*. If used extensively or inappropriately, BROWN may convey excessive needs suggesting insecurity.

BLACK is the negation of color and conveys a sense of *nothingness*, of extinction. It is associated with night, with the unknown, and with fear and evil. Luscher states that preference for BLACK indicates a wish to "renounce everything out of a stubborn protest against the existing state in which one feels that nothing is as it should be" (p. 80). Extensive or inappropriate use relates to feelings of strong dissatisfaction, dysphoria, and depression.

Many of the colors have expected or ordinary usage, e.g., RED for chimneys, GREEN for leaves, BROWN for tree trunks, and BLACK for the outline of objects. Moderate usage for these features does not convey the above connotations.

☐ Interpretation of Structural Characteristics as Related to Features

Each of the PDs (both achromatic and chromatic)—HOUSE, TREE, PER-SON, PERSON OF THE OPPOSITE SEX, and ANIMAL—can be analyzed in detail with regard to the subjective connotation of each of its features. These features elicit reactions which by their experiential, symbolic, or metaphoric nature reflect particular characteristics of the self or selfobject representations. The interpretation of these features is modified or amplified by the way in which they are drawn, i.e., by their *structural* characteristics. For example, if the door of the HOUSE evokes a subjective sense of accessibility, then how lightly or darkly its lines are drawn, can provide us with a sense of the drawer's uncertainty or tension about someone gaining access to him or her. The interpretation of the structural characteristics discussed in the previous section—line quality and shading, placement, and color—apply in essence to the analysis of the features as they do to the drawings as a whole.

The relevant features of each of the PDs will be identified and elaborated upon in terms of the experiential quality that each feature adds to the understanding of the self or selfobject represented by the drawing.

Kohut (1977) discussed the psychopathology of the narcissistic personality disorders as consisting of: (1) *primary defects*, acquired in childhood, in the psychological structure of the self, e.g., deficits in self-esteem, self-soothing, etc. and, (2) *secondary structure-formations*, also built in early childhood, which he called defensive and compensatory structures.

a) *Defensive:* When its sole or predominant function is the covering over of the primary defect in the self, e.g., repression, suppression, and denial.

b) *Compensatory:* Rather than merely covering a defect, it compensates for this defect. It develops on its own and functionally rehabilitates the self by making up for the weakness in one pole of the personality, e.g., the area of exhibitionistic and ambitious needs, by strengthening another pole, e.g., the area of idealizing needs.

Examining the features of the drawings in terms of their structural characteristics provide the examiner with a picture of the primary defects and the defensive and compensatory secondary structures that the individual has developed to reconstitute the self.

How the drawer represents the various features—line quality, size, choice of colors, etc.—conveys to and elicits or evokes from the examiner a sense of the felt experience of the drawer.

This map of the structure of the self will include not only defects and defensive and compensatory structures but the identification of healthy structures which are functioning in an *optimal* manner.

CHAPTER

Structural Analysis–The House

The relevant features of the House include:

A   The Door
B.   The Walkway
C.   The Baseline and Grounding
D.   The Windows
E.   The Walls
F.   The Roof
G.   The Chimney
H.   The Surroundings
I.   Other Features

☐ A. The DOOR

This feature evokes the subjective connotation of permitting others to gain access to where one lives and also of permitting egress from the HOUSE—of gaining access to the world. The characteristic thus related to the self (or ascribed to the relevant selfobject) may be termed *accessibility*.

Omission

Omission of the door from the drawing of the HOUSE evokes a sense of severe *resistance* to letting others in or letting oneself out, of isolating or withdrawing the self (or experiencing the selfobject in this way). Drawing a door without a *doorknob* conveys a feeling of uncertainty or ambivalence with regard to letting others gain access.

Connection of Door to Base of HOUSE

Ordinarily the door is drawn flush with the baseline. Not doing so again conveys the feeling of someone who is unsure or *ambivalent* about whether he desires to facilitate ingress or egress.

Size

Large size, (i.e., the door is disproportionately too big for the size of the wall it is on), conveys a sense of *overcompensation for underlying anxiety* with regard to being accessible by exaggerating one's openness to contact resulting in *overeagerness* for contact.

Small size, (i.e., the door is disproportionately too little for the size of the wall it is on), conveys a feeling of *resistance* about letting others in.

Detailing

Ordinarily the door is drawn with only the detail of the doorknob. Other details may include designs, panels, porticos, framing, columns, windows, a mailbox, knockers, numbers, signs, bells, or steps. As the number of details *increase*, the sense is of *preoccupation or concern* about becoming accessible. If even one detail is *very carefully* drawn it may indicate a *compulsive compensation* for this concern; if the detail(s) is (are) elaborately drawn, the presence of *compensatory exhibitionism* may be inferred.

Extra Doors

Drawing other than a single main door, e.g., double doors, a back or side door, also conveys a sense of subjective difficulty with the easy and direct flow of entering or leaving the HOUSE. *Double doors* suggest *overcompensation*. *Other doors, in addition* to the main entrance, may indicate *uncertainty* with regard to the manner in which one wishes to become accessible, i.e., directly or obliquely; or, they may reflect the drawer's need for another avenue of egress.

If *only a side* door is drawn, the feeling evoked is one of *ambivalence*; if only a back door is indicated, it is of strong *reluctance* or *guardedness* with regard to becoming accessible to others.

Blocked Door

If the door is blocked by, e.g., grass, foliage, flowers, a railing, a fence, or some other obstruction, the feeling evoked is of *reluctance* or *ambivalence* about being accessible.

Optimal Accessibility

The impression that the door has been drawn in a way that expresses a sense of *optimal* accessibility can be inferred if *all* of the following formal conditions are met for *both* achromatic and chromatic drawings:

> a *single* (not a double) door;
> *moderate* line quality and/or shading;
> *moderate* size (proportionate to the size of the wall it is on);
> door has a *doorknob* and possibly *one or two details* that are not *overly carefully or elaborately* drawn;
> is the *only* door drawn;
> is *connected* to the baseline;
> is on the *main* (largest or most prominent) wall;
> is *not blocked.*

☐ B. The WALKWAY

Often, a path leading outward from the door, steps, or baseline is drawn. The subjective connotation that is evoked is one of *approachability,* i.e., the drawer is indicating a feeling of reaching out, of making contact with others.

Omission

Not drawing a walkway suggests that the drawer defines the task in a more restricted or limited way than someone who does draw one. The connotation is of a more *passive or avoidant* attitude toward the issue of being approached.

Length and Width

A walkway that is either proportionately *too long* or *too short* evokes a feeling of *ambivalence* about being approached as does one that is *narrow* throughout most of its length. Walkways that are *narrower at the junction* with the HOUSE than at the *end* suggest a feeling of *initial openness with*

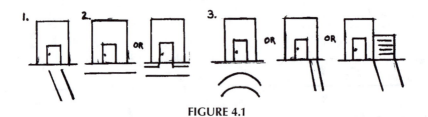

FIGURE 4.1

increased hesitancy the closer one gets; on the other hand, walkways that are *narrower at the end than at the junction* with the HOUSE suggest *initial hesitancy with increased acceptance* as one gets closer.

Connection to House

Walkways that are 1) *disconnected* from the HOUSE, 2) *run parallel* to it, or 3) *end at some other terminus*, all convey a feeling of *ambivalence* about being approached (see Figure 4.1).

Straightness

A walkway that is *curved or angled* at least 90 degrees and has its *terminus face the side of the page* rather than the bottom evokes a feeling of *ambivalence*.

Optimal Approachability

This may be inferred if the walkway meets *all* of the following conditions for *both* the achromatic and chromatic drawings:

walkway has *moderate* line quality and/or shading;
has *moderate* length and width (proportionately long in relation to the size of the HOUSE and approximately as wide or wider than the main door extending through the length of the walkway);
is *connected* to the HOUSE at the main door;
is *mostly straight or curved less than 90 degrees and terminates facing the bottom* of the page.

☐ C. The BASELINE AND GROUNDING

The *baseline* refers to the *bottom edge* of the HOUSE. *Grounding* refers to any implication that the HOUSE is *attached to the ground*. It may be represented by: 1) a baseline for the HOUSE that extends past the sides of the

HOUSE *or* a line below the baseline that extends beyond the sides which represents the ground, 2) an imaginary line suggested by the presence of groundcover such as grass, shrubs, flowers, or trees, or 3) a horizon line or mountains in the background of the HOUSE (see Figure 4.2).

The manner in which the HOUSE is attached to its base and its base to the ground refer, subjectively, to an inner sense of *stability*, of how connected to reality, how "based or grounded" the drawer feels him/herself (or a significant selfobject) to be.

Omission

Where the HOUSE is drawn with *neither a baseline nor grounding*, the sense is of someone with a *severe problem in connecting to the real world*, i.e., someone whose perceptions and judgment are influenced more by inner concerns than by an awareness of the need to connect to the real world. (This does not apply to a drawing where the grounding obscures the baseline or a groundline serves as a baseline.)

Where *there is a baseline but there is no indication of any grounding*—as if the HOUSE were "floating in air"—the sense is of a subjective feeling of *instability*, of having no connection with a source of reality confirmation.

Connection of Baseline and/or Grounding to the HOUSE

Where only some of the vertical wall lines or only part of the baseline *make contact* with the grounding, we have a sense of the drawer's *felt instability*. This feeling may also be ascribed to the situation where the base of the page is used as a baseline. When the HOUSE is drawn with *all* of the vertical lines *not touching the baseline* or, if the baseline is omitted, all of the vertical lines *end above the grounding*, the feeling is of a person whose sense of self (or experience of the selfobject) *is not well grounded in reality*.

Optimal Stability

An optimal sense of feelings of stability can be inferred if *all* of the following conditions are met for *both* achromatic and chromatic drawings:

FIGURE 4.2

both a baseline to the HOUSE and grounding for the HOUSE are *present*;
both have *moderate* line quality and/or shading;
colors used for grounding are *appropriate*, e.g., grass is green and not red;
the baseline *connects* with the grounding;
all of the vertical wall lines of the HOUSE *touch* the baseline.

☐ D. The WINDOWS

Windows evoke the subjective experience of *relatedness*. From within the HOUSE one is able to look out into the environment but one can also be seen from without. Windows thus convey a sense of the capacity of the self or selfobject to relate back and forth or *interact* with the surroundings.

Omission

The failure to draw any windows evokes a feeling of *severe withdrawal*—a sense that one is shut off from the environment.

Number and Location

One window located on the walls only (as opposed to other parts of the HOUSE only) suggests a *limited or ambivalent* feeling with regard to interacting with the world. (This does not apply if the one window is a substantially large window.)

More than five windows located on the walls only, implies *anxiety* about relating with an effort to *overcompensate* for it.

Any number of windows located on the walls but *only above the top of the door* evokes a sense of *guardedness*. The windows should be located *either totally below or above and below the top of the door* (see Figure 4.3).

If windows are *mainly* drawn on the *roof*, a feeling of *privacy* is evoked, of being able to see out but not having others be able to see within. If the windows are *only* drawn on the roof, this feeling is intensified as well as evoking a sense of *isolation or withdrawal*.

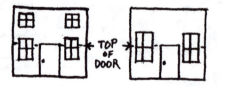 

FIGURE 4.3

Size

Large size, (i.e., the windows are disproportionately too big for the size of the wall the windows are on), conveys a sense of *overcompensation for underlying anxiety* with regard to relating to the world.

Small size, (i.e., the windows are disproportionately too little for the size of the wall the windows are on), conveys a feeling of *resistance* to interacting with others.

Detailing

This refers to any addition beyond the lines drawn to indicate the out-line and inner panes of the windows. Details include shades, shutters, curtains, flowerpots or boxes, or people or animals seen through the windows.

When *no* details are added, i.e., only lines indicating panes are drawn, the sense is of a *passive* or "no frills" approach to relating to the environment.

When at least *one* detail is added (that does not block the window), the sense is of an attempt to more *actively* personalize one's involvement with the environment.

Where windows are *blocked or barred*, a feeling of *guardedness* is evoked.

Bare windows, i.e., windows drawn with a single line as outline, either as square, rectangle, or circle, convey a sense of *emptiness or guardedness,* or of *impulsivity or bluntness* if they are hastily or carelessly drawn.

Optimal Relatedness

This can be inferred if *all* of the following conditions are met for *both* achromatic and chromatic drawings:

> *between 2 and 5* windows (or one large window);
> windows have *moderate* line quality and/or shading;
> moderate size (proportionate to the size of the wall they are on);
> are located *on the walls* of the HOUSE (as well as the roof, door, or garage but *not only* on the roof, door, or garage);
> are located *not only above the door;*
> have at least *some* detailing without being *blocked or barred.*

☐ E. The WALLS

This includes two components—the vertical and horizontal lines used to represent the edges of the walls and the area within those lines.

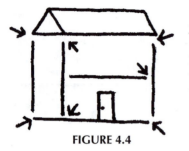

FIGURE 4.4

The walls of the HOUSE can be felt, subjectively, to be the container of the self (or selfobject), i.e., that which keeps what is inside secure from both inner disruption or outer threat. In that, walls may be thought of as an expression of *self-control*.

Omission

It is relatively rare for a HOUSE to be drawn with no indication of lines used to represent the edges of the walls. In those instances where other features are drawn but nothing indicating a containing structure, the sense is of *massive lack or loss of control with severe reality distortion*. This should be weighted in terms of the drawer's awareness and intention, e.g., the stated attempt to present an "abstract" representation of a HOUSE.

Connectedness

Where *most or all* of the points of juncture are left open, i.e., not connected, the sense is of a carelessness or overlooking of a significant aspect vital to the structural integrity of the HOUSE. This elicits a sense of *loosening of control* with the implication that *unplanned or unwanted behavior* may be manifested (see Figure 4.4).

Straightness

Wall lines that are relatively *curved or slanted* convey a sense of insecurity with concurrent *lessened self-control*.

Transparency

FIGURE 4.5

When the drawer reveals what is inside the HOUSE, i.e., objects can be viewed as if the walls were *transparent*, the subjective sense is of a disregard of reality with the implication of *loss of control over cognitive capacity*, i.e., the possibility of a severely regressed state thought disorder (see Figure 4.5).

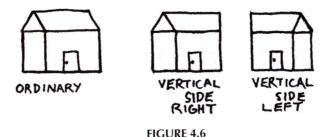

ORDINARY   VERTICAL   VERTICAL
                  SIDE   SIDE
                 RIGHT   LEFT

FIGURE 4.6

Detailing

Occasionally, the walls are filled in with *bricks, stones, or logs*. When this is done in an *overly careful or elaborate* manner, the feeling elicited is one of a preoccupation and involvement with relatively small component elements. The inference is of a need to reinforce the containing aspect of the HOUSE, possibly a *compulsion* to shore up one's sense of self-control.

House Sides

Ordinarily, the HOUSE is drawn with neither of the sides drawn as a vertical line including the roof, wall, and/or chimney. When the HOUSE is drawn with a *vertical* side, (either depicted or using the edge of the page as a side), the subjective feeling is of a cutting-off, a *suppressing* of the normal flow of the HOUSE. This evokes a sense of the drawer's *insecurity* and *need to control* inner processes.

If the vertical side is on the *right*, the insecurity may relate to issues dealing with the *future*.

If the vertical side is on the *left*, the insecurity may relate to issues dealing with the *past* (see Figure 4.6).

Perspective

When only a 1) *single wall* (with or without roof) is depicted, the sense is of the drawer giving only a *limited or superficial* view of himself in order to maintain control over what is expressed or perceived (see Figure 4.7(1)).

Where a 2) *wall within a wall or several floors* are drawn but still only in the context of a *single* side being shown, the sense is of the drawer attempting to give a sense of depth but still *not providing real perspective* (see Figure 4.7(2)).

The drawing of 3) *both end walls* as well as a facing wall ("double perspective") suggests that the drawer does not have a grasp of realistic per-

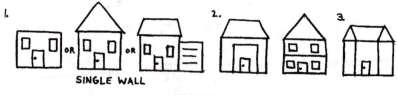

SINGLE WALL

FIGURE 4.7

spective (see Figure 4.7(3)). This may infer a possible *neurological, cognitive, or thought disorder*. If these can be ruled out, the sense is of someone who may want to be seen in depth but manifests the desire in a regressively concrete mode, inferring underlying *fear and guardedness*.

Optimal Self-Control

This can be inferred when *all* of the following conditions have been met for *both* achromatic and chromatic drawings:

> walls have *moderate* line quality and/or shading;
> *all or most* of the meeting points of the wall lines *connect* with other wall lines, roof line, and baseline;
> wall lines are relatively *straight*;
> walls are *not transparent*;
> detailing is *not* done in an *overly careful or elaborate* manner;
> there are at least *two* walls;
> *both* end walls are *not* drawn;
> *neither* of the sides are drawn as a *vertical* line including the roof, wall, and/or chimney;
> the HOUSE is drawn with an indication of *three dimensions* (depth, width, and height).

☐ F. The ROOF

The roof, as the top of the HOUSE, does not subjectively relate to one's sense of relatedness and interaction with the world. People do not ordinarily live in the roof area; it is a place to store things (memories). As such, it appears to refer to *inner cognitive processes*—ideation, memory, fantasy—that relate more to the inner self than to the outer world.

Omission

The failure to draw a roof on the HOUSE elicits the feeling of the drawer *shutting off* (either *suppressing or repressing*) this aspect of self-experience (see Figure 4.8).

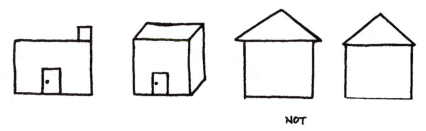

NOT

FIGURE 4.8

Size

A *large* roof, (i.e., disproportionately too wide *or* too high for the size of the HOUSE), suggests a preoccupation with the part of the self that is involved with inner cognitive processes.

A *very large* roof, (i.e., disproportionately too wide *and* too high for the size of the HOUSE, suggests *excessive preoccupation*, i.e., *obsessiveness*, with regard to inner cognitive processes.

A *small* roof, (i.e., disproportionately too narrow *or* too low for the size of the HOUSE), connotes *limited or constricted* involvement with inner cognitive processes.

A *very small* roof, (i.e., disproportionately too narrow *and* too low for the size of the HOUSE), connotes very constricted involvement or *severe avoidance, suppression, or repression* of inner cognitive processes.

Where a HOUSE is drawn *only as a roof* ("roof-walling"), the feeling that is elicited is of a person who relates to the environment with *excessive reference* to his own inner cognitive processes and has limited awareness of or input from the environment (see Figure 4.9).

Detailing

Similar to the walls, the roof is occasionally drawn with all or most of the area filled in with *shingles or planks*. When this is done in an *overly careful or elaborate* manner, the feeling elicited is of a need to *reinforce the containment* of inner cognitive processes via *obsessive-compulsive* mechanisms.

Placement

If the roof is *cut off by* or *touches the top* of the page, the sense is of the drawer's need to "put a lid" on his thoughts, i.e., to either *repress or suppress* inner cognitive processes.

FIGURE 4.9

Split Roof

Where the roof is *divided* into *two or more* segments or *separate* roofs are drawn on different parts of the HOUSE, the sense is of a *splitting* of inner cognitive processes with the the possibility of the drawer being *dissociated* from significant parts of these processes.

Optimal Inner Cognitive Process

This can be inferred when *all* of the following conditions have been met for *both* achromatic and chromatic drawings:

> roof has *moderate* size (is proportionate in height and width to the size of the HOUSE it tops);
> has *moderate* line quality and/or shading;
> its detailing is *not done in an overly careful or elaborate* manner;
> is *not cut off or touching* the top of the page;
> is *not divided* into *two or more* segments.

☐ G. The CHIMNEY

The chimney is frequently included in the drawing of the HOUSE. The subjective connotation evoked points toward the drawer imagining a fireplace or stove within the HOUSE. This leads to a feeling of benign human activity, e.g., cooking or lighting a fire in the fireplace, which elicit feelings of nurturance, nourishment, companionship, contentment, and tradition—in short, associations around the idea of *warm familial involvement*. The chimney by itself suggests the *potential* for such involvement. If *smoke* is also drawn, the vicarious sense of the *fulfillment* of these potentials within the self (or in a selfobject) may be experienced.

Omission

If *both* the chimney and smoke are omitted, the sense is of *avoidance* on the drawer's part of associations related to warm familial involvement. If the chimney is drawn but *without smoke*, the feeling evoked relates to the awareness of, or potential for, such involvement but with a sense of *unfulfillment*, of incompleteness.

Size

A *chimney* that is *too small* for the size of the roof suggests *anxiety* about the potential for warm familial involvement while one that is *too large* connotes *exhibitionistic compensation* for that anxiety.

Too little smoke conveys a feeling of *disappointment or dysphoria* with regard to realizing the potential for warm familial involvement, while too much smoke evokes a sense of *anxiety or flooding* with regard to how the drawer experiences his familial interactions.

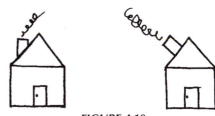

FIGURE 4.10

Detailing

The chimney is frequently drawn with *all or most of the bricks* outlined. If this is done in an *overly careful or elaborate* manner, the sense is of *obsessive* preoccupation with issues pertaining to warm familial interaction.

Chimney Roof Angled

Normally, the chimney is drawn in a *vertical* position. When it is drawn in the direction of the *slant* of the roof, the implication is of a cognitive deficit with the possibility of a *neurological disorder* (see Figure 4.10).

Optimal Warm Familial Involvement

This can be inferred when *all* of the following conditions have met for *both* achromatic and chromatic drawings:

> chimney has *moderate* size (is proportionate to the size of the roof it is on or proportionate to the size of the HOUSE if it is drawn along the side) which indicates the *potential* for optimally warm familial involvement;
>
> *realization* of that potential is indicated if a *moderate* amount of *smoke* is coming from the chimney (proportionate to the size of the HOUSE and the chimney);
>
> *moderate* line quality and/or shading for both chimney and smoke;
>
> *colors* used for chimney and smoke are *appropriate*, e.g., black or red for chimney and black for smoke;
>
> detailing is *not done in an overly careful or elaborate* manner;
>
> chimney is drawn *vertically*.

☐ H. The SURROUNDINGS

Occasionally, the drawer will surround the HOUSE with *additional objects*, e.g., people, animals, tools, toys, toolsheds, the sun, clouds, etc. More often *foliage*, e.g., grass, shrubs, flowers, and trees will be added. The implication is of someone who interprets the instructions to draw a HOUSE in an expansive rather than a literal or constricted manner—conveying a sense of *involvement and vitality.*

Omission

Omission of additional objects is not particularly unusual; the content of what is drawn may add a particular understanding to what the drawer subjectively experiences with regard to self (or selfobject) involvement with others. For example, it is unusual for adults to draw the *sun*. Inclusion evokes the sense of a person who is relating to the task in a more *childlike or regressive* manner. It suggests the need or wish for the presence of a powerful parental selfobject.

Omission of any kind of foliage is less usual. A *moderate* amount of grass, shrubbery, and/or trees brings a sense of *life or vitality* to the drawing. A *limited* amount elicits a feeling of *limitation* with regard to felt vitality; an *extensive* amount suggests an *exhibitionistic overcompensation* for a subjective experience of limited felt vitality. The presence of a *tree whose branches appear to overhang* the HOUSE or which *dominate* the HOUSE may connote the drawer's subjective experience of a *powerful parental selfobject who shelters and/or dominates* the self.

☐ I. OTHER FEATURES

Garage and Driveway

Occasionally, a *garage* is drawn, either as an addition to or contained within the structure of the HOUSE. A *driveway* may or may not be added. Implicitly, this connotes the importance of the car to the drawer, either as a way of leaving the HOUSE or, via the driveway, of increasing accessibility to others. The feeling thus evoked is an enhanced sense of *involvement* with the environment.

Unusualness

An *unusual response* to the request to "draw a house" that is not in compliance with the request, e.g., a blueprint or multiple houses, elicits a feeling of the drawer's need to structure the world in her own terms, implying an attitude of *negativism toward authority or oppositionalism. Blueprints* convey an additional feeling of *intellectualism. Drawing more than one HOUSE* elicits feelings of *inner confusion or splitting* with regard to one's core identity.

Inquiry

The drawer is asked to respond to two questions: "Who lives in the house?" and "What feelings does it give you?" (or "What do you get from the house?").

The answer to the first helps us to determine whether the drawing of the HOUSE refers primarily to a *self*-experience or is the greater emphasis on the drawer's experience of the *selfobject* qualities associated with the HOUSE. The answer also provides a sense of the drawer's relatedness or involvement with others.

If the response is that *he and his family* live in the HOUSE, or *he and another person(s)*, the connotation is that the drawing refers to *both* experiences related to the self and the significant selfobject milieu provided by the drawer's family. The implication is of an *optimal* balance of relatedness between self and selfobject(s).

If the response refers *only to a family or couple without specific reference to the drawer*, the emphasis shifts to the *selfobject*. Here, the sense is of an *overemphasis or reliance* on the selfobject.

If the response is, "I live in the house," with no reference to anyone else, the focus would appear to be the self with a feeling of *withdrawal, detachment, or isolation* from selfobject involvement.

If the response is "One person," with no reference to the self, the focus would appear to be a *specific selfobject*, again with a feeling of *over involvement with a selfobject* and a corresponding *deemphasis on the self*.

If the drawer answers that the house is *unoccupied*, the connotation is of *self-alienation and detachment* from involvement with selfobject(s). The feeling elicited is one of *felt barrenness and depression*.

To the second question, a *positive* response, i.e., one that employs *affirmative* adjectives, e.g., "happy" and "pleasant," elicits feelings of an *optimal* self or selfobject evaluation.

A *negative* response, i.e., one that employs *dysphoric* adjectives, e.g., "sad" and "empty," elicits a feeling of *depressiveness*.

A *bizarre* response, i.e., any expression that conveys an *eccentric or very unusual* feeling about the HOUSE, e.g., "crazy" and "weird," elicits the sense of the drawer's difficulty in experiencing herself (or the selfobject) in a *realistic* manner.

A *mixed* response, i.e., the drawer responds with *both positive and negative* adjectives, conveys a sense of *ambivalence* about the self (or selfobject).

Responses that are *neutral or unclear* do not provide a sense of the drawer's affective self or selfobject evaluation.

☐ An Example of a Structural Analysis of the House

The Case of X. N.

X. N.s TREE drawings were used to exemplify an impressionistic analysis. Here, his HOUSE drawings will be used to illustrate a structural analysis.

Examining the achromatic HOUSE (Figure 4.11) drawn shortly after X. N. began therapy, we see that the door appears to be rather large for the wall it is on, suggesting a tendency toward overcompensating for underlying anxiety with regard to becoming accessible to others. The line quality is heavy, further indicating some degree of tension. The door is not fully connected to the baseline which conveys a feeling of ambivalence about being accessible.

The omission of a walkway indicates a passive or avoidant stance with regard to being approached.

While the HOUSE has a reinforced baseline, there is no indication of it being grounded, pointing to a subjective sense of instability. The rather faint line quality of the baseline furthers the impression of X. N.s uncertain sense of stability.

The presence of three windows and their positioning below the top of the door indicates that while X. N. may have difficulty being accessible and approachable, he wants to relate or interact with others. However, the mix of heavy and faint line quality of the windows conveys a sense of X. N.s outward tension and inner uncertainty about relating. Also, their excessive size suggests an overcompensation for anxiety about relating. The presence of windows on the roof evokes a feeling of a need for privacy. The lack of details on the windows furthers the picture of passivity with regard to interacting with others.

The line quality of the wall lines again shows a mixture of tension and uncertainty, in this case about self-control. However, the lines are for the most part connected and straight, pointing to an adequate sense of self-control. This is borne out by the three-dimensional perspective. However, there is a loss of perspective in the drawing of the porch covering the main wall's door and windows. This suggests difficulty with feelings of control in relation to both being accessible and relating to others.

The roof appears to be somewhat large, suggesting a tendency to be overly involved with inner thoughts.

FIGURE 4.11

The rather small chimney points to trepidation about the potential for warm familial involvement. The absence of smoke evokes X. N.'s sense of unfulfillment in this area. The weak sketchy line quality adds to a sense of uncertainty about reaching this goal.

The absence of additional objects or any sign of foliage conveys a feeling of lifelessness, emptiness—a lack of felt vitality.

Looking at the HOUSE as a whole, it is placed above the midline suggesting evasion of the here-and-now with a corresponding excessive use of fantasy. Its rather substantial size, however, conveys the feeling that X. N.'s basic sense of adequacy is intact.

X. N.'s response that only he lives in the HOUSE underscores the sense that the drawing relates primarily to his own feelings of withdrawal, detachment, and isolation from others. The fact that he responds to the question of what feeling the HOUSE evokes with the answer, "warmth," suggests that he has an underlying belief in his capacity for connectedness with a responsive selfobject (see Figure 4.11).

The chromatic HOUSE (Color Plate 11) appears structurally to be very similar to the achromatic drawing. Here, though, the heavily shaded red door stands out in conveying a sense of tension accompanying an active, striving desire to be accessible. Although it is connected to a baseline it is still some distant from the ground which coincides with the ambivalence found in the pencil drawing. The somewhat carelessly drawn porch lines, which encase the door, add to a sense that there is uncertainty about becoming accessible to others. Nevertheless, the vividness of the color evokes the sense of X. N.'s powerful underlying preoccupation with allowing other people to have access to his inner self.

Three outstanding additional features of the color drawing attract our attention: 1) The heavily drawn yellow of the windows, which elaborates the feeling obtained from the achromatic drawing that X. N. wishes to interact but has considerable anxiety, resulting in overcompensation and ambivalence. The heavy pressure that he used to fill in the window area gives us a sense of his excessive desire for relatedness and possibly the pressure he may feel to achieve it; 2) Similarly, the large size of the chimney and heavily drawn red shading of it reveal the underlying pressure and drive that he experiences in striving to achieve warm familial relatedness. It is as if what he conceals from himself on a conscious level (achromatic drawing) comes to light when given the opportunity for affective expression (chromatic drawing); 3) In this vein, the addition of the green grass grounding connotes X. N.'s subjective sense of stability and vitality on the deeper, affective level.

Figure 4.12 (achromatic HOUSE) and Color Plate 12 (chromatic HOUSE) show X. N.'s drawings of a HOUSE after approximately four years of biweekly therapy. Compared to the first set of drawings, we find drastic changes, almost as if they were done by a different person.

Beginning the structural analysis of both the achromatic and chromatic drawings, with an examination of the door, we find a near-optimal level of accessibility—the single door has mostly moderate line quality in the pencil drawing and moderate shading in the crayon drawing. Both have a doorknob and the pencil HOUSE has a window. On both drawings it is the only door drawn and is not blocked. The achromatic door is connected to the baseline while the chromatic door is slightly separated from the steps. However, the softly modulated blue color conveys a sense of calmness and tranquility. Only in terms of size do we find a trace of the overcompensation for anxiety that was evident in the first set. X. N. may

FIGURE 4.12

manifest this to a greater degree when exposed to a more affective dimension of experience.

While he still does not draw a walkway, X. N. adds steps to his HOUSE, which enhance the subjective sense of his readiness to facilitate ingress. The heavy line quality of both pencil and crayon drawings, and the partially darkened shading of the latter, evoke a sense of tenseness accompanying his permitting greater approach and access.

We also see significant change in the moderate line quality of the baseline of both achromatic and chromatic drawings and in the addition of foliage, objects, and a groundline to the pencil drawing, giving a real sense of groundedness for the HOUSE. The impression of a strong sense of stability, of being firmly grounded and connected to the world, is highly prominent in the achromatic drawing representing the patient's day-to-day involvement and it is somewhat present but with more anxiety, on a deeper, affective level. With regard to the experience of relatedness as reflected by the windows, X. N. seems overly eager to interact as evidenced by the large number and size in both drawings. Moderate line quality in both, and especially, the soft, modulated use of yellow in the color drawing, suggests an absence of tension and a presence of hopeful anticipation, affectively. The impression is of "someone being home." The roof windows on both drawings are done with the kind of dimensionality that evoke a sense of careful perspective in viewing the environment from a safe vantage point.

The subtle detailing of the walls on the achromatic HOUSE and the softly modulated shading in the chromatic drawing provide a sense of calm inner self-control. Some tension may be experienced with regard to the interface with the outside world as reflected by the heavier pressure with which he drew the vertical wall lines. However, the connectedness of the meeting points, the straightness of the lines, and the general sense of perspective all convey an overall strong sense of self-control.

The line quality, shading, and detailing of the roof convey a sense of peaceful, easy involvement with inner cognitive processes as represented by the roof. The modulated red color of the color drawing suggests that X. N.'s fantasies may have to do with success and achievement. Although prominent, the roof appears to be proportionate to the size of the HOUSE in the achromatic drawing but to be somewhat overflowing in the chromatic drawing. Possibly, X. N. has better integration when dealing with practical reality (achromatic), then when exposed to a more affective level of experience (chromatic).

This may also be evidenced by the existence of chimneys with smoke coming out of them in the pencil drawing but no chimney in the crayon drawing. Drawing two chimneys, which is unusual, and very light lines for the smoke, suggest that X. N. may be ambivalent or uncertain about his familial involvements but ready to tackle them on a practical level while being avoidant on an affective level. This is in marked contrast to the large, prominent, heavily shaded chimney of the first chromatic drawing.

The inclusion of lawn furniture and a swimming pool in the pencil drawing convey a sense of comfort and fun. The heavy line quality of the lawn furniture of the crayon drawing betrays a feeling of tension when relating to these needs on a more affective level. The amount and variety of the pencil foliage evoke an optimal sense of vitality, which is more limited and more intense on the deeper affective level.

The inquiry still points to X. N.'s solitary status but with a greater sense of self-acceptance, i.e., the achromatic HOUSE is "warm and cozy" and the chromatic HOUSE has "lots of sunshine coming in—warm and comfortable inside." (Responses to the first drawings were "warmth" and "comfort," respectively.)

The structural analysis provides a comprehensive picture of the patient's movement during the space of four years, some of which may be attributable to psychotherapy. He appears to have become less anxious and uncertain about becoming accessible to others and, to a lesser degree, more approachable. There seems to be a clear improvement in the extent and quality of his relatedness as well as a subtler, more modulated sense of self-control along with a strong sense of stability in day-to-day affairs. From excessive fantasy we appear to find a blend of fantasy with awareness and focus on the outside world. In the area of familial involvement, there appears to be less anxiety and avoidance on a behavioral level with avoidance replacing overriding anxiety on an affective level. (X. N. achieved a form of rapprochement with his children from his first marriage, but continued to feel unfulfilled emotionally in his relations with them.) Finally, the sense of self-acceptance, involvement with life, and of vitality seemed to be clearly demonstrated by the changes from the first to the second set. The contrast between the achromatic and chromatic drawings within and between each set added a rich dimension to the analysis of the different levels of X. N.'s life experience. While he appears to have integrated much positive change in his ability to function in the practical, day-to-day world, the color drawing allows for the expression of continued anxiety about the self and selfobject connections that the achromatic drawing alone does not provide.

CHAPTER

Structural Analysis–The Tree

The relevant features of the TREE include:

A. The Branch and Leaf Area (BL area)
B. The Trunk
C. The Roots and Grounding
D. The Surroundings
E. Other Features

A. The BRANCH AND LEAF AREA

The BL area of the TREE relates, in a subjective sense, to a reaching out to the world. Branches are often referred to as the "arms" of the TREE. The drawer conveys a sense, by how she represents this feature, of how she experiences *interaction* with the environment.

Omission

It is very unusual for the TREE to be drawn without branches or an outline of an area, which suggests with greater or lesser detail, branches and/or the leaves or foliage covering them. Doing this evokes a feeling of *severe inhibition* with relation to how the person experiences interaction with the world. It has the further connotation of a *withdrawn, depressive* sense of the self or the selfobject that the TREE represents (see Figure 5.1).

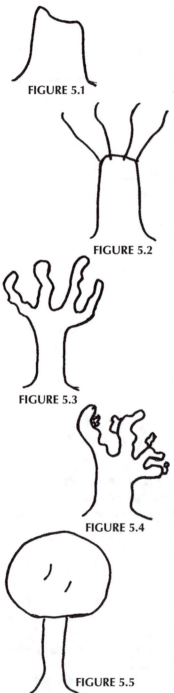

FIGURE 5.1

FIGURE 5.2

FIGURE 5.3

FIGURE 5.4

FIGURE 5.5

Size

Large size, (i.e., the BL area is proportionately too big for the size of the trunk and roots), conveys a sense of *overcompensating for anxiety* about interacting with the environment. This may take the form of *excessive activity*.

Small size, (i.e., the BL area is proportionately too small for the size of the trunk and roots), evokes a sense of *passivity and inhibition*, a lessening of active reaching out.

Detailing

One-dimensional branches with no leaves convey a feeling of *inadequacy* about interacting (see Figure 5.2).

Similarly, drawing *bare branches*, (i.e., two-dimensional but with no leaf or foliage cover), evokes a sense of *barrenness*, of having little to offer with regard to interacting with others (see Figure 5.3).

An *unclear BL area*, (i.e., no definable outline or inner area), also conveys a sense of *inadequacy* (see Figure 5.4).

Where *only an outline* is drawn, (i.e., branches, leaves, or other objects are not depicted - the interior is virtually empty), the feeling is of a *limition* of interaction, of intentionally *shutting off* or having an *oppositional* attitude toward interaction with the world (see Figure 5.5).

Branches and/or leaves that are *broken or bent* evoke a feeling of being *damaged* or *handicapped* in one's ability to interact; the corresponding affect has a *depressive* tone (see Figure 5.6).

Branches and/or leaves that are shaped like *sharp, pointed spikes or fingers,* or that are drawn as *clubs,* convey a feeling of *hostility*—an attitude toward interaction that has an *aggressive* connotation (see Figure 5.7).

When branches are drawn as two-dimensional with the *far end open* with no foliage covering the open end, the connotation is of an *inability to contain or control* one's affect or behavior (see Figure 5.8).

In contrast, where branches are *separately surrounded by foliage*, (i.e., they appear to be "wrapped in cotton"), the sense is of one's *inhibiting* oneself in terms of interaction with others (see Figure 5.9).

Branches that are *long and thin, pointing upward or turned inward,* evoke a feeling of *inhibited* interaction where the person is withdrawing into himself, possibly with *compensatory fantasy* (see Figure 5.10).

Where branches and/or leaves *touch (or nearly touch) the ground,* (the TREE may be identified as a "weeping willow"), the feeling is of *inhibited* interaction with *depressive* affect (see Figure 5.11).

When leaves or fruit are depicted as *falling or fallen* (shown on the ground), a sense of a *loosening of affect* accompanying the process of interaction, is evoked (see Figure 5.12).

When branches are drawn on the *trunk below the BL area*, the sense is of someone reaching out from an inappropriate place, of *immaturity or regressiveness* (see Figure 5.13).

Branches that are drawn as *new growth extending from a barren trunk* convey a sense of *inchoateness*, a feeling of *tentative striving* to overcome feelings of doubt about one's adequacy (see Figure 5.14).

Where branches and/or leaves or fruit are drawn in a *very detailed, careful, or repetitive* manner, the feeling is of the drawer needing to *control* his interaction—of *compensating for anxiety with compulsive behavior*; where

FIGURE 5.6

OR

FIGURE 5.7

FIGURE 5.8

FIGURE 5.9

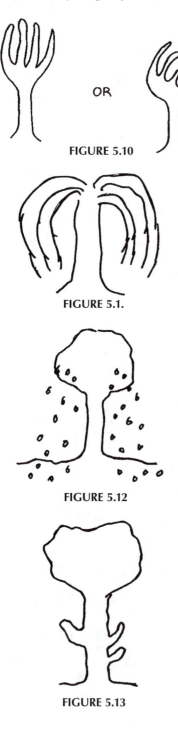

OR

FIGURE 5.10

FIGURE 5.1.

FIGURE 5.12

FIGURE 5.13

the details are *elaborately* drawn, *compensatory exhibitionism* may be inferred (see Figure 5.15).

Finally, when the BL area is drawn in a perfectly (or near perfect) *symmetrical* manner, the impression is of the drawer's need to *compensate for ambivalence or uncertainty* with regard to interacting with the environment by *striving to maintain perfect balance* (see Figure 5.16).

Configuration

Where the BL area is drawn with an *overemphasis to the right*, (i.e., the trunk may be vertical or slanted but the BL area extends markedly further from it to the right side or is more heavily shaded, outlined, or elaborated on the right side), the inference is that *anxiety* about interacting with the world is inducing an *avoidance of the here-and-now* with a possible *preoccupation with the future* with corresponding *fantasy and ideation*.

Where the BL area is drawn with an *overemphasis to the left*, the inference is that the anxiety about direct interaction induces an *avoidance of the present*, with a possible *preoccupation with the past*, with a *lessening of intellectual controls* and corresponding *regressive behavior*.

Drawing the top of the BL area as *flat* evokes a feeling of *suppressing* reaching out to the world with corresponding *depressive* affect (see Figure 5.17).

When the outline of the BL area is drawn as a *curlicue*, the sense is of a *hurried, impatient, superficial* way of interacting with the environment (see Figure 5.18).

Placement

When the outline of the BL area *touches or comes close to the edge of the page but clearly does not extend over or off the edge,* the feeling conveyed is of someone who has an urge to *reach beyond the limits* of her environment but *contains or constricts* herself.

Extending the BL area *past the top or side of the page* so that part of it is clearly cut off conveys a sense of *defying environmental restrictions or limits* in response to one's feelings of *constriction* with regard to interacting.

FIGURE 5.14

FIGURE 5.15

Additional Objects

When other objects, e.g., *fruit, flowers, birds, nests, animals, swings,* etc., are drawn in addition to or instead of branches and leaves, the sense is of a *compensation for anxiety* about interacting with the world with a focus on what transpires *within* the confines of the structure. These additional objects are found more often in the drawings of children than of adults. This infers the presence of *regressive wishes or fantasies. Fruit,* in particular, elicits a sense of *nurturance*—to feed or be fed.

FIGURE 5.16

Optimal Interaction

The impression that the BL area has been drawn in a way that expresses a sense of *optimal* interaction with the environment can be inferred if *all* of the following conditions for *both* the achromatic and chromatic drawings are met:

FIGURE 5.17

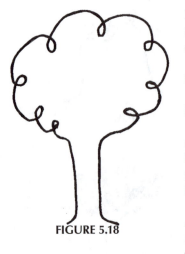

FIGURE 5.18

BL area has *moderate* line quality and/or shading;

colors used are appropriate for the season named;

it has *moderate* size (proportionate to the size of the trunk and roots);

it has *one- or two-dimensional, moderately shaped* branches and/or leaves; *mostly* covered by foliage or an outline filled in by foliage; the branches, if outlined, are not shaped like *sharp, pointed spikes* or like *clubs,* are *not broken or bent*, do *not point upward, inward, or touch the ground, do not emanate from the lower part of the trunk,* and are *not* drawn in a *very detailed, careful, repetitive, or overly elaborate* manner;

it is *not overemphasized to either side*;

it is *not perfectly symmetrical*;

it is *not drawn flat on the top*;

the outline is not drawn as a *curlicue*;

it does *not come close, touch,* or *extend over the edges* of the page; and

it has *no additional objects.*

☐ B. The TRUNK

The trunk relates, in a subjective sense, to the drawer's feelings of *inner strength* (or that of a significant selfobject). The trunk emerges from the earth and supports the BL area; the vicarious sense is of one's *capacity to "stand-in-the-world."*

Omission

FIGURE 5.19

The trunk is rarely omitted in the drawing of the TREE. If this is done, the sense is one of *severe feelings of insufficiency or inadequacy.* It evokes feelings of *inhibition, passivity,* and *avoidance* (see Figure 5.19).

Size

When the trunk is *overly wide,* (i.e., disproportionately too wide for the width of the BL area

BENT

SLANTED
OR LEANING

CURVED

FIGURE 5.20

and the roots), the feeling conveyed is one of *overcompensation for anxiety* about a lack of inner strength. "Me thinks the drawer protests too much," i.e., adopts an overly *grandiose-exhibitionistic* stance.

Overly narrow trunk size, (i.e., disproportionately too narrow for the width of the BL area and the roots), evokes feelings of *inner weakness* with a correspondingly *inhibited* stance in the world.

Overly tall trunk size, (i.e., disproportionately too high for the height of the BL area), conveys a feeling of *overcompensation for anxiety* about inner weakness. If the trunk cannot be seen because it is partially covered by the BL area, the drawer may be experiencing or perceiving underlying *anxiety* which she feels *ambivalent* about revealing; if the trunk is shown uncovered, the connotation is of a *grandiose-exhibitionistic compensation*.

Where the trunk is *overly short* (i.e., disproportionately too low for the height of the BL area), the feeling elicited is of *inadequate strength* with a tendency to adopt a *passive* stance.

Structure

When the trunk is drawn as noticeably *bent, slanted, leaning, or curved* (i.e., not standing relatively perpendicular to the ground), the vicarious experience is one of a *damaged* sense of inner strength or a feeling of being *weighted down*. Where the trunk turns toward the ground, the inescapable affective tone is one of *depressiveness* (see Figure 5.20).

A *split trunk* (i.e., drawn as veering off from a base in two or more directions), conveys a feeling of *confusion* about how to express or

FIGURE 5.21

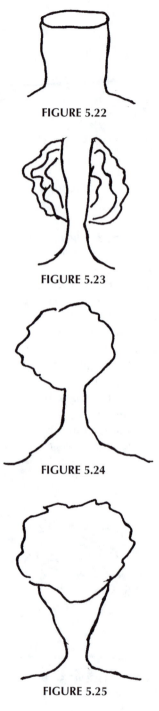

FIGURE 5.22

FIGURE 5.23

FIGURE 5.24

FIGURE 5.25

direct one's sense of inner strength, about how to position oneself in the world with the effect of a *split* in the sense of self (see Figure 5.21).

When the trunk is drawn as a *stump with no growth coming from it,* the feeling is of *severe felt weakness, withdrawal, and depressiveness* (see Figure 5.22).

A trunk that is *open at the top* (i.e., it extends through the BL area), evokes a feeling that the drawer's preoccupation with his inner strength dominates his interactive functioning, suggesting the *domination of fantasy over activity* (see Figure 5.23).

A trunk that is *very broad at the base with diminishing breadth* conveys a feeling of a *lessening of confidence* in one's strength as one approaches the need to interact with the environment, possibly involving feelings of *inhibition* (see Figure 5.24).

A trunk that is *narrower at the base than where it joins the BL area* conveys the opposite feeling—*basic anxiety* about one's inner strength *overcompensated for by grandiose* feelings as one approaches the need to relate to the world (see Figure 5.25).

Finally, where the trunk is drawn as *one-dimensional* (i.e., using a single line), the feeling conveyed is of *severe felt inadequacy* with regard to one's sense of inner strength (see Figure 5.26).

Knothole

Knotholes, or circles drawn on the face of the trunk or along its side, are sometimes included, more frequently by children but also by adults. If the trunk subjectively relates to felt inner strength, the knothole may relate to modifications of this experience.

A knothole that *bisects* the trunk (i.e., cuts it by touching or almost touching the sides of the trunk), suggests a crippling interruption in the integrity of the trunk and may represent the expression of a *traumatic event* in the life of the drawer that led to a sense of *damage* to one's feeling of inner strength.

When the knothole appears to *gouge out a side* of the trunk, the sense is of a trauma that left the person feeling *physically damaged.*

Where the knothole is positioned on the trunk may indicate at what *age* the trauma occurred. For example, if the trunk as a whole represents the person's actual age, e.g., 30, then if the knothole is placed about one-third of the way up, the significant event may have occurred around the age of 10.

FIGURE 5.26

Depicting an animal in the knothole gives a feeling of a need for a place of safety, a place to withdraw into. As such it elicits a feeling of *compensating for feelings of damaged strength by regressive thoughts or actions.*

Optimal Sense of Inner Strength

For the drawing of the trunk to convey an *optimal* sense of inner strength, *all* of the following conditions for *both* the achromatic and chromatic drawings should be met:

> Trunk has *moderate* line quality and/or shading;
> *colors* used are *appropriate*, e.g., brown or black, not red;
> it has *moderate* size (proportionate to the size of the BL area and roots);
> it is *not bent, slanted, or curved* but is relatively *perpendicular* to the ground;
> it is *not split, drawn as a stump, open at the top, broader at the base or top*, but is relatively *even* throughout its length;
> it is *two-dimensional (not drawn as a single line)*; and
> it does *not have a knothole.*

☐ C. The ROOTS AND GROUNDING

This refers to some indication that the TREE is attached to the ground—is not simply "floating in the air." *Grounding* may be indicated by a *root structure* that appears to merge with the ground. It may also appear as an extension of *one or both lines of the edges of the trunk,* which extend out from the trunk in a mostly horizontal manner; and/or it may be shown as a separate *groundline,* either touching the base of the TREE or be below it;

FIGURE 5.27

or the groundline may be shown as a *horizon line* which appears to be behind the TREE. Finally, it may be implied by the presence of other *foliage*, e.g., grass, bushes or as objects (e.g., fallen fruit or leaves) (see Figure 5.27).

The feelings associated with the roots and grounding of the TREE are similar to those related to the baseline and grounding of the HOUSE, i.e., a sense of *stability*, of how connected the drawer feels to a source of realistic footing (or perceives a significant selfobject to be). The presence of roots adds a further dimension to the vicarious sense of what the drawer experiences as he includes this feature. It conveys a feeling of someone who has a more differentiated appreciation of his antecedents—what he comes from, i.e., how his capacity to interact with the world and feeling of inner strength emerge from the soil, from what lies under the surface—one's genetic and biological roots, one's "inner self" that may be out of conscious awareness.

Thus, the drawing of roots, in addition to the subjective connotation of stability, suggests a sense of *connectedness with one's inner self* (or the perception of that quality in a significant selfobject).

Omission

Where the TREE is drawn with *none* of the above indications of roots *and* grounding, (or is not drawn with the bottom of the page as a base), the feeling evoked is of someone who does not experience a connection with her inner self or something that confirms her stance in reality. Consequent feelings elicited are ones of *instability and insecurity*.

Omitting roots but providing some other source of grounding evokes a feeling of being *cut off from one's inner self but having some sense of stability*.

Connectedness of Groundline

When the TREE is *above* a groundline (appears to be floating above the ground), the feeling evoked is of having *uncertain contact with reality* with the consequent experience of *instability and insecurity*.

Where the *base of the page* is used as grounding, the feeling of needing an external source to provide stability and security is elicited, suggesting an *immature, regressive, or dependent* sense of self.

FIGURE 5.28

Root Structure

Roots that are drawn as *thin and making poor contact* with the grounding evoke a feeling of *faltering connectedness*, of someone struggling to find something to enhance the sense of being securely attached to one's inner self and to reality (see Figure 5.28).

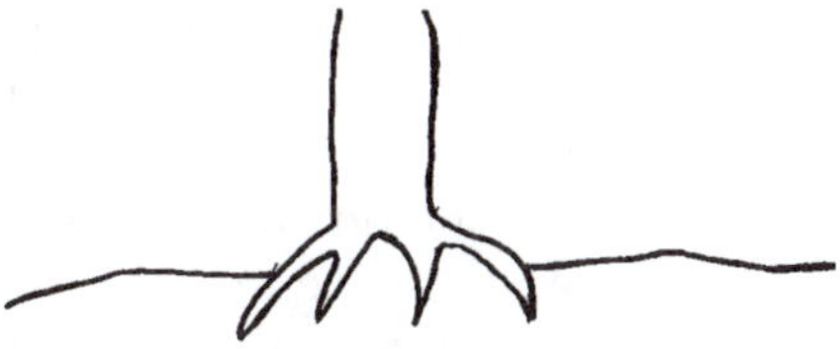

FIGURE 5.29

Roots that are drawn like *claws or talons* elicit a sense of someone whose experience of being grounded in reality and whose inner awareness is tenuous and who *compensated* by adopting a *hostile-aggressive* stance (see Figure 5.29).

When roots are drawn in a *transparent* fashion, i.e., are cut off by the groundline but can be seen even though they are underground, the feeling is of a disregard of reality that implies a *loss of control over cognitive functioning*, i.e., the possibility of a thought disorder (see Figure 5.30).

Optimal Stability and Inner Connectedness

For the drawing of roots and grounding to convey a sense of optimal stability and connectedness, *all* of the following conditions for *both* the achromatic and chromatic drawings should be met:

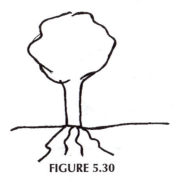

> The TREE should have *roots that merge with the ground and some other form of grounding*, e.g., extensions of line(s) of the trunk, a groundline, a horizon line, other foliage, or objects;
> roots and grounding have *moderate line quality and/or shading*;
> *colors* used for roots and grounding are *appropriate*; e.g., brown or black

FIGURE 5.30

for roots, green for grass, any color for flowers;
there is *moderate* size of root structure and other forms of grounding;
roots should *make contact* with the groundline (if drawn) and should
    not be drawn as *claws or talons* and should *not be transparent*; and
the *bottom of the page* should *not* be used as grounding.

☐ D. The SURROUNDINGS

The drawer may include *additional objects* not physically connected to the
TREE, e.g., the sun, clouds, people, animals, houses, tools, toys, other
foliage (bushes, flowers), etc. Similar to the HOUSE, the subjective connotation is of *expansiveness, involvement, and vitality.*

Omission of additional objects is more often the case than not. However,
specific objects elicit different subjective meanings. For example, the *sun*
is frequently found in the drawing of children. If drawn by an adult, the
sense is of someone who may feel the need to include the powerful, life-
giving source, i.e., the parental selfobject. This conveys feelings of *regressive or dependent wishes or needs.*

Clouds and/or birds, which are *freely and moderately* drawn, elicit a sense
of *vitality,* of an *alive connection to nature.* However, if they are *heavily* drawn,
the feeling is one of *anxiety or tension* concerning that which surrounds
the self (or selfobject).

Other foliage such as shrubs or flowers also convey feelings of *aliveness,
vitality,* and involvement with the surroundings, if they are *moderately*
drawn.

People, animals, or other physical objects suggest *preoccupation or anxiety* with
regard to particular selfobjects in the environment.

☐ E. OTHER FEATURES

Unusualness

A TREE that is drawn like a *keyhole,* i.e., the outline only in the shape of
a keyhole, evokes feelings of *avoidance and
oppositionalism* (see Figure 5.31).

Multiple TREES elicit feelings of *inner division,*
of a *split* sense of self.

Inquiry

FIGURE 5.31

The drawer is asked to respond to three questions:

1) How old is the tree?
2) Is it alive or dead?
3) What season of the year is it in?

The *age* of the TREE relates to the drawer's subjective experience of his (or the selfobject's) relative *maturity*.

If the age given is *within five years,* plus or minus, of the drawer's real age, an *optimal* sense of maturity may be inferred.

If the age given is *more than five years* less than the drawer's real age (or he answers, "young" or "very young"), the feeling evoked is of a *diminished* sense of felt maturity, the more intense the further from the actual age.

If the age given is *more than five years over* the drawer's real age, he may experience *anxiety* about his felt maturity and may be attempting to *compensate* for these feelings.

If the drawer states that the TREE is *100 years or more* (or is "old" or "very old"), the feeling evoked is one of *diminished capacity* with accompanying *depressiveness*.

The answers with regard to whether the TREE is *alive or dead* and to what season it is depicted as being in, relate subjectively, to the drawer's sense of *vitality* (or that of a significant selfobject).

The usual response is "*alive.*" Any deviation, e.g., "half-alive" or "mostly alive," elicits a sense of the drawer's diminished sense of vitality. A response of "*dead,*" (or "dying" or "half-dead"), relates subjectively to severely *diminished vitality* with accompanying *depressiveness*.

If the response is given that the TREE is "*artificial,*" the feeling evoked is one of *inauthenticity,* of feeling fraudulent, of not having a real sense of one's place in the world.

With reference to the *seasons, spring* evokes a feeling of *hopeful anticipation*. *Summer* gives an *optimal* sense of being vitally alive. *Autumn (or fall)* convey a feeling of *ripening,* of *maturity,* but also a bittersweet awareness of the *passing or lessening* of one's optimal vitality. *Winter* suggests the feeling of a shutting down of the self, of *barrenness* and possible *depressiveness*. Drawing a Christmas tree may be an attempt to *compensate* for these feelings with *regressive or dependent* wishes.

The drawer should be questioned as to whether the time of the year when the drawings were administered influenced her decision regarding choice of season.

☐ An Example of a Structural Analysis of the TREE

The Case of I. D.

I. D., a 46-year-old recently divorced man, entered therapy with feelings of anxiety and depression. In addition to his failed marriage, he had been recently victimized by "corporate downsizing" and was in the process of being phased out of his middle-management position with a large corporation.

Projective drawings were administered within the first month of therapy. The BL area of the achromatic TREE (Figure 5.32) appears to be large with respect to the trunk suggesting that I. D. is overcompensating for anxiety with regard to interacting with the environment. The looping "curlicue" lines representing the foliage calls to mind a kind of frenzied, haphazard approach. In terms of line quality, the loops go from dark to light indicating the alternating state of his mood—tension and uncertainty going round and round with no clear sense of order or direction. The greater preponderance of area covered on the right side indicates preoccupation with what lies ahead—the future. There is a sense of trailing off on the left side, which may parallel his feelings regarding his failed marriage and career. The single heavily drawn vertical line to the left of center in the BL area may relate to the strong affect accompanying his wish to cut himself off from his past.

The trunk is of relatively moderate size but is quite barren looking. The heavier line on the left side may indicate the tension and anxiety accompanying the strength needed to deal with the past. This is in marked contrast with the rather faint line on the right side. This line is slanted inward and is not connected to the branch extending to the right. The strong sense is of feelings of lack of strength, and of hesitancy and uncertainty in dealing with the future.

FIGURE 5.32

There is no indication of roots and the merest of lines suggesting grounding. The overall impression is of a person with no sense of stability, security, or connection with his inner self.

The overall size of the TREE and its approach to the edge of the page points to I. D.'s urge to reach beyond the limits he encounters in his day-to-day reality and experiences within himself.

The inquiry reveals that he sees his achromatic TREE as "very mature," approximately his own age, alive, and in summer. This may attest to his need to shore up his beleaguered sense of self by idealizing it on a conscious level.

When we examine the chromatic TREE (Color Plate 13), done in the same sitting, it is as if it were drawn by a different person. This TREE really looks like a mature, vitally alive specimen. The BL area is well-balanced, proportionate to the size of the trunk, more carefully and moderately shaded in appropriate colors. The branches blend into the foliage. Looking closely, we can see more dense shading on the right side indicating more energy needed to interact with what lies ahead. The single heavy black line going to the right may also reflect the tension he feels in this regard.

The trunk appears strong and sturdy. It is moderately and sensitively shaded in appropriate colors. When given the opportunity for affective expression, I. D. reveals an optimal sense of inner strength.

There is an indication of roots merging into a grounding of moderately shaded, appropriate color, providing an optimal sense of stability and connectedness.

Similar to the achromatic TREE, the chromatic TREE is rather large and approaches but does not go over the edge of the page. Again, we have the sense of a person who wants to be noticed (mirrored) and who contains himself from reaching beyond the limits of his environment. Further, the chromatic TREE is depicted in the inquiry as mature and full of vitality, "standing on two feet in the park." In this case, unlike the pencil TREE, we have a strong sense of the inherent affective capacity of I. D., given the opportunity to express himself on a deeper, affective level. These two drawings reinforce the need to provide such range of opportunity in utilizing PDs. In I. D.'s case, it indicates that he is experiencing considerable stress and self-doubt in the more limited, day-to-day practical world represented by the achromatic drawing but has a strong basic self-image and inner reserves, when functioning in an environment that provides a full range of expressive potentials represented by the chromatic drawing.

Figure 5.33 and Color Plate 14, are I. D.'s achromatic and chromatic TREE drawings, respectively, done after approximately one year in therapy.

The BL area of the pencil drawing is oddly shaped, with a protrusion dipping downward on the right side. The heavy, crimped line quality and shading on the left side suggest the tension and avoidant wishes experienced in interacting with what remains of his past life. The more sketchy, flowing, and moderate line quality on the right side evoke a more uncertain, unfocused feeling. The section heading downward suggests a dropping off of interactive energy.

The trunk seems to be poorly integrated with considerable sketchy shading suggesting a beleaguered sense of inner capability. The trunk appears

FIGURE 5.33

to extend quite a distance into the BL area conveying the feeling that I. D. is more connected with his basic capacity to stand in the world than to interact in it.

Although there is a groundline, the trunk is not connected to it indicating that a sense of groundedness in the practical world is now present, but is far from providing a full sense of stability and security.

The smaller size of the achromatic TREE, as compared to the initial pencil drawing, suggests that I. D. has retreated from the over-compensatory, overly active position he adopted at the beginning of therapy. He definitely seems to be more in touch with his anxiety and dysphoria, the latter evidenced by his giving the age of the TREE as "100." He retains his feeling of aliveness but this is tempered by his awareness of the passing of time (season is given as "fall") and his sense of being in a transition period between a troublesome past and an uncertain future.

Again, the chromatic TREE is a vast improvement over the achromatic one, but is not as vibrant as the first chromatic TREE.

The foliage of the BL area is generally balanced but there is some extension on the right side. Also, the branches extend down the trunk on this side. The impression is of a lack of integration or a splitting from the branches that veer off to the left. The overall sense is of a more solid capacity to deal with the past than with the future. The trunk, however, appears to fade on the left and toward the bottom. Possibly, I. D. can interact more effectively with past issues but experiences a sapping of inner energy as a result. The heavy black line of the trunk on the right may represent a need to shore himself up to deal with the future. The reinforced root on the right side appears to add to the picture of I. D.'s sense of tension in newly establishing his base of stability. The heavy green line which cuts off the trunk at the base, violating realistic representation, gives a sense of the strong anxiety accompanying issues of stability and dealing with one's inner self.

The introduction of red and orange into the BL area may indicate I. D.'s increased awareness of excitement and action as well as ambivalence in his interaction with others.

Similar to the achromatic TREE, the color TREE is "100, alive, in the fall." Compared to the beginning of therapy, the chromatic TREE, while still more sturdy and powerful looking than its pencil counterpart, reflects I. D.'s uncertain and unsettled affective state.

It should be noted that the patient was in the throes of trying to establish a business at the time of the second set of drawings. He also had very limited social involvements. It appears that I. D.'s TREE drawings reflect both a more differentiated and complex sense of self on the day-to-day, practical level and a more uncertain, less secure sense on the affective level.

6

CHAPTER

Structural Analysis–The Persons–Male and Female

The relevant features of the person and the person of the opposite sex include:

A. The Head
B. The Torso
C. The Limbs
D. The Whole Person
E. Other Features

 ## A. The HEAD

This feature relates, for the drawer, to a number of different subjective experiences depending on which part or characteristic is focused upon.

1) The Entire Head

When one considers the whole head by itself, the subjective connection is to the drawer's experience of her *cognitive capacity* (or that of the relevant selfobject). This includes *intellectual adequacy* and *fantasy activity*. "Having a good head on one's shoulders," generally implies being intelligent, perceptive, and able to problem solve. "His head is in the clouds," suggests a person who is overideational or embedded in fantasy.

71

Omission

When the head is *concealed*, e.g., behind an object, the sense is of someone who is *highly anxious* about his cognitive functioning with a tendency to *withdraw from active involvement with the world.*

Not drawing the head at all is quite unusual. Here, the sense is of a *profound disturbance* regarding one's cognitive capacities. This suggests the possibility of a *thought and/or neurological disorder.*

Size and Shape

An *overly large* head, (i.e., head is disproportionately long and/or wide relative to the size of the body), conveys a sense of *overcompensation for anxiety* with regard to cognitive capacities. This may involve *exhibitionistic* behavior with regard to cognitive skills and/or a tendency to be *over ideational.*

An *overly small* head, (i.e., head is disproportionately short and/or narrow relative to the size of the body), conveys a sense of *felt inadequacy* with consequent *passive, inhibited,* or *withdrawn* behavior related to intellectual expression or *repression or suppression* of inner processes.

A head that has *irregular contours* or a *distinct geometric shape other than oval or round* of *any size* elicits feelings of *distortions* with regard to one's cognitive capacities. The possibility of a *thought and/or neurological disorder* is raised (see Figure 6.1).

Connection of Head to Body

When the *head is not connected to the body*, i.e., appears to be "floating," and there is no indication of a neck, the feeling is of *severe disturbance* in one's sense of how one's cognitive capacity relates to the rest of the body, i.e., a breakdown of mind-body integrity, with the possibility of a *thought and/or neurological disorder.*

2) The Face as a Whole

Drawing the face and its features, including hair, focuses the drawer on how he appears to others. Subjectively, this relates to a *concern about appearance*, i.e., how presentable one is to others and what others can read into one's expression. Additionally, each facial feature has a subjective connotation related to its particular function.

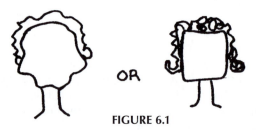

FIGURE 6.1

Position

When the head is presented as a *rear view*, i.e., only the *back of the head* is shown and the face cannot be seen, the sense is of someone who does not want to "face the world." This conveys extreme anxiety about one's appearance with consequent *hypersensitivity, inhibition*, and *withdrawal* from contact.

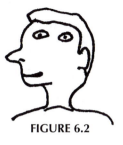

FIGURE 6.2

When the face is presented in *profile*, the sense is of a person whose concern about his/her appearance induces a turning away from direct contact. This elicits feelings of *evasiveness or avoidance*.

When the face is presented as a *confused profile*, i.e., some features are in profile and some are front view, the sense is of *severe disturbance* with regard to appearance suggestive of a possible *thought and/or neurological disorder* (see Figure 6.2).

Facial Hair

The inclusion of a *mustache and/or beard* on the male figure may relate to a specific feature of the self or a selfobject. In some cases it may reveal *anxiety* about appearance in terms of *pleasantness, strength, or masculinity*. The facial hair may represent an effort to *compensate for felt inadequacy*.

3) Eyes

The eyes are a person's "windows to the world." They receive information but also reflect attitude and mood. Like the windows of the HOUSE, they are a major conduit of how one *relates* to others. "The gleam in the mother's eye" is the metaphor for the process of "mirroring," i.e., the affirmation of one's grandiose self by the all-important selfobject, so necessary for the development of a healthy self-structure. Thus, the eyes have tremendous significance for the individual in terms of how one *receives and reacts to affective stimuli* from the selfobject milieu and how a person experiences her own capacity to convey affective states to others.

Omission

If *both eyes are not drawn*, the feeling is of *severe anxiety* with regard to receiving from and expressing affect to others. The sense is of *severe withdrawal* with a possible *thought and/or neurological disorder*.

If *only one eye is drawn* (in a full-face presentation), the sense is of *ambivalence* about receiving and reacting to affective stimuli with both *withdrawal and awareness* tendencies.

If *one or both eyes are concealed,* e.g., by hair or a hat, the sense is of *anxiety* leading to *avoidance* with regard to receiving or conveying affective stimuli.

Size

Overly large eyes, (i.e., eyes are disproportionately large relative to the size of the head), convey a feeling of *hypersensitivity* with regard to receiving or conveying affective stimuli.

Overly small eyes, (i.e., eyes are disproportionately small relative to the size of the head), elicit feelings of *avoidance and withdrawal.*

It should be noted that eyes of any size that are *heavily drawn or reinforced,* convey feelings of *anxiety and tension* about receiving and conveying affective stimuli that suggest *suspiciousness and guardedness* with the possibility of a *paranoid* reaction.

Shape and Composition

Eyes that are drawn as an *outline with only pupils omitted,* e.g., as empty circles or ovals or as eyeglasses only with the eyes not drawn, convey a sense of emptiness, of not wanting to see or be seen, i.e., of *withdrawing* into the self.

Where eyes are drawn as *dots or circles totally filled-in,* as *slits,* i.e., as *single lines* or *with very narrow openings,* or as *closed,* i.e., only eyelids or eyelashes are shown, the sense is also of someone *severely restricting* the ability to receive or convey affective impressions.

Where *eyelids and/or eyelashes* are drawn the feeling is of *preoccupation or sensitivity* with regard to receiving and conveying affective stimuli. If *very carefully or elaborately* drawn, the implication is of *obsessive-compulsive or exhibitionistic* tendencies, respectively.

Eyebrows

When eyebrows are shown, their *shape* augments the interpretation of the drawer's subjective position with regard to receiving or conveying affective stimuli.

FIGURE 6.3   **FIGURE 6.4**   **FIGURE 6.5**

If drawn *slanted toward the nose*, as if "frowning," the sense is of a *hostile* attitude (see Figure 6.3).

If drawn in a *semicircular* fashion, as if *"raised" or "arched,"* the sense is of a *disdainful* attitude (see Figure 6.4).

If drawn in a *thick or heavy* way, the sense is of an *aggressive* attitude (see Figure 6.5).

4) Ears

Similar to the eyes, the ears subjectively relate to the individual's *reception of and reaction to affective stimuli.*

Omission

Omitting the ears by *not drawing* them on a figure fully facing front elicits a sense of *withdrawal, (severe, if both ears)*, as a way of dealing with anxiety about receiving affective stimuli.

Concealing one or both ears by hair or a hat, or by angling the head, elicits the feeling that this anxiety is dealt with by *evasiveness or avoidance.*

Size

Overly large ears, (i.e., ears are disproportionately large relative to the size of the head), convey a feeling of *hypersensitivity.*

Overly small ears, (i.e., ears are disproportionately small relative to the size of the head), elicit a sense of *avoidance* of stimulation and *withdrawal* into the self.

As with the eyes, ears of any size that are *heavily drawn or reinforced* elicit feelings of anxiety that may be dealt with by *suspiciousness and guardedness* with the implication of *paranoid* tendencies.

Earrings

The addition of earrings to a male or female figure appears to relate more to *concern about appearance* than to reception of emotional stimuli. If *very carefully or elaborately* drawn, the suggestion is of *obsessive-compulsive or exhibitionistic* reactions, respectively. If drawn on a male, one would have to consider the entire manner and identification of the figure drawn, to sense whether the drawer was expressing an *oppositional* attitude.

5) Nose

The nose has the subjective connotation of *both concern about appearance and how one receives and reacts to affective stimuli* from the environment.

"Being nosy," "sticking one's nose into other peoples business," "having a nose for news," are all expressions attesting to this latter quality. These also imply an *assertive* dimension to this feature. The expression, "sniffing out the dirt" conveys the primitive aspect of the sense of smell that may also be experienced in the way one relates, affectively, to others.

Omission

Not drawing a nose conveys a sense of *serious disturbance* with regard to how one appears to others and how one receives and reacts to affective stimuli. This kind of reality denial has a *primitive* feel suggesting a more severe *avoidant* reaction.

Size

An *overly large* nose, (i.e., the nose is disproportionately large relative to the size of the head), may relate to the drawer's *hypersensitivity* about his appearance and receiving stimuli. It may then infer an *overly assertive compensation* for these feelings in terms of how the individual relates to the environment.

When the nose is drawn with *nostrils specifically depicted*, the sense is of a more *primitive, aggressive* way of interacting (see Figure 6.6).

An *overly small* nose, (i.e., the nose is disproportionately small relative to the size of the head), elicits a sense of *avoidance and passivity* with regard to one's appearance and to receiving and reacting to affective stimuli.

FIGURE 6.6

6) Mouth

The mouth is the basic organ for receiving from and communicating with the world. What one receives relates to fundamental issues of survival, nourishment, and growth. As such, it has strong affective significance. In like manner, how one verbalizes one's inner self-state is vital for establishing and attuning self-selfobject interrelatedness. In drawing the mouth the individual thus expresses feelings related to *affective interaction* with sources of selfobject gratification.

Omission

Not including the mouth in the drawing of the face connotes a *severe deficit* in affective interaction, a *felt incapacity to make contact*. As such it elicits a sense of someone who experiences him/herself as severely cut-off from significant others, i.e., *profoundly withdrawn*. This implies an affect state of *severe depressiveness*.

Size

An *overly large* mouth, (i.e., the mouth is disproportion- ately large relative to the size of the head), conveys a sense of *anxiety* about af- fectively interacting with important selfobjects. Draw-

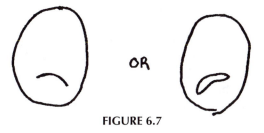

FIGURE 6.7

ing a large mouth brings to mind the expression, "That person has a big mouth." In other words, the individual *compensates* by taking an *overly active, assertive, or aggressive* approach.

An *overly small* mouth, (i.e., the mouth is disproportionately small rela- tive to the size of the head), conveys a sense of the drawer's minimizing the extent of affective interaction by *avoiding or withdrawing* from contact with consequent feelings of *helplessness and hopelessness*, i.e., *depressiveness*.

Expression

When the mouth is drawn as a *single line which is "unsmiling,"* i.e., drawn straight, not turned up or down at the corners, the feeling is of *impassive- ness*, of adopting a noncommittal, nonrevealing position with regard to affective interaction.

A *single line drawn as a downward slash or a full mouth drawn as "sneering,"* i.e., one corner turned down, conveys a feeling of *hostile aggressiveness* (see Figure 6.7).

A *single line drawn as "grinning,"* i.e., exaggeratedly upturned at the cor- ners, conveys the sense of an attempt to *overcompensate for anxiety* about interacting by appearing to be *overly eager to engage*.

A *full mouth drawn as an open, empty circle or oval* evokes a sense of *help- less passivity* with regard to affective interaction.

Additional Objects

Drawing a *cigarette, cigar, or pipe* in the mouth conveys a sense of the drawer's involvement with a direct source of oral (selfobject) gratifica- tion. As such, it may represent an *overcompensation for anxiety* about re- ceiving affective supplies by *adopting a pose of self-sufficiency*.

7) Teeth

Teeth are ordinarily not drawn. When specifically depicted, the drawer may be expressing a need to *compensate for anxiety* about receiving and expressing affective needs.

When teeth are drawn in a *very detailed, careful* fashion, the sense is of an *obsessive-compulsive* reaction.

When teeth are drawn with *heavy line quality*, the sense is of *tension* with regard to affective interaction which may be relieved by *aggressiveness*. This also applies to teeth drawn in a *jagged* manner.

When teeth are drawn in *outline but in a faint* manner, the sense is of *uncertainty and tentativeness* about receiving and expressing emotional needs.

Drawing *one or a few teeth spaced* conveys a sense of *immaturity and regressiveness* with regard to affective interaction.

8) Chin

The chin involves, subjectively, a sense of *assertiveness*, of risk-taking. The expression, "sticking one's chin out," conveys this sense of taking action, of being willing to take a stand.

Omission

Not drawing a chin conveys a feeling of *severe passivity, of avoiding and withdrawing* from taking an assertive stance.

Size

An *overly large* chin, (i.e., the chin is disproportionately large relative to the size of the head), elicits a sense of the drawer *overcompensating for anxiety* about being assertive with the possibility of *overly assertive or aggressive* reactions.

An *overly small* chin, (i.e., the chin is disproportionately small relative to the size of the head), conveys the feeling of *passivity and withdrawal* from opportunities for assertiveness.

9) Hair

Hair is often referred to as a person's "crowning glory." As such it conveys a sense of how important to the individual this feature is with regard to his/her appearance to others with particular reference to how *attractive or sexually desirable* one is. Hair thus relates to grandiose-exhibitionistic strivings involving fantasy and/or behavior. The covering of the hair by Orthodox Jewish women exemplifies this interpretation in that only one's approved sexual partner, the husband, may directly observe one's natural hair.

Omission

Not drawing hair has varying subjective connotations, depending on the gender of the figure drawn and the gender of the drawer. In any case, it conveys a sense of *anxiety about sexual desirability* with a rather extreme reaction of *avoidance* in dealing with it.

Extent

FIGURE 6.8

Excessive hair, (i.e., hair is disproportionately excessive or extensive relative to the size of the head), elicits a sense of the drawer's *overcompensating for anxiety* about his sexual attractiveness by *overly active, assertive, or aggressive behavior* or *fantasizing* such behavior.

Limited hair, (i.e., hair is disproportionately limited or sparse relative to the size of the head), conveys the sense of the individual's *passive or inhibited* reaction with regard to feelings of sexual desirability.

FIGURE 6.9

Additional Characteristics

Bizarre hair, i.e., very rare or unusual hairstyle, provides a sense of the attempt to *overcompensate for anxiety* about sexual desirability by *denying* the need to *conform* to accepted standards. This implies *oppositional* tendencies (see Figure 6.8).

Disheveled or messy hair conveys a sense of *low self-esteem* with regard to sexual attractiveness with consequent *dysphoric* feelings (see Figure 6.9).

Hat

Drawing a hat conveys the feeling that the drawer attempts to *defend* against anxiety about sexual attractiveness by *covering or concealing* her feelings, thoughts, or fantasies. However, one would have to consider the identification of the figure drawn, e.g., cowboy or policeman, to determine whether, or to what degree, the hat expresses the drawer's defensive needs or has another connotation.

The *size* of the hat conveys the same implications for relating to anxiety about sexual attractiveness as does the *extent* of the hair.

Optimal Expressiveness with Regard to the Head

The subjective connotations related to the drawing of the head vary when considering the head-as-a-whole and its subfeatures. To be considered an *optimal* expression of the drawer's inner experience, *all* of the following conditions have to be met for *both* the achromatic and chromatic drawings.

With regard to the *entire head,* the feeling evoked relates to the drawer's sense of his (or that of the relevant selfobject's) *cognitive capacity* including *intellectual adequacy and fantasy activity.* Here, an *optimal* presentation of the whole head would involve:

> *moderate* line quality and shading;
> *appropriate color* used for the outline, i.e., black, brown, yellow, orange, red, not blue, green, or purple;
> *moderate* size (proportionate to the size of the body);
> *oval or round* shape;
> *connection* of head to body.

When considering the *face-as-a-whole,* the subjective sense relates to a *concern about how one appears to others.* (The *nose* and *earrings* also relate to this concern.) Here, an *optimal* expression would involve:

> *face* is presented in full, *front view or slightly angled;*
> *face* has *moderate* line quality and shading;
> *color(s)* used for shading of face are *appropriate* (see *"entire head"*);
> *face* has no *facial hair;*
> *nose* has *moderate* line quality and shading;
> *nose* is of *moderate* size (proportionate to size of head);
> *earrings* (if present) are of *moderate* line quality, size, and shape.

The *eyes and ears* relate to the drawer's feelings concerning *receiving and reacting to affective stimuli.* (The *eyes,* additionally, provide a sense of the person's capacity to *convey* affective states.)

Optimally, the drawing of these features would have the following characteristics:

> *both eyes and both ears are shown;*
> *eyes and ears* have *moderate* line quality and shading;
> *color(s)* used for *eyes* are *appropriate*—all but red, orange, or yellow;
> *color(s)* used for *ears* are *appropriate*—all but blue, green, or purple;
> *eyes and ears* are of *moderate* size (proportionate to size of head);
> *eyes* are drawn with an *outline and pupil, not as dots or circles totally filled-in, slits, or closed;*
> *eyebrows* (if drawn) are *slightly arched* and have *moderate* line quality and shading, are *not slanted or fully semicircular.*

The *mouth* expresses feelings related to *affective interaction.* Optimally, the mouth would involve:

> *moderate* line quality and shading;
> *appropriate color,* e.g., *all* but blue, green, or purple;

moderate size (proportionate to the size of the head);

an expression that has an *upper and lower lip* (either separate of connected but not an open, empty circle) or if drawn as a *single line is
turned upward at the corners;*

no cigarette, cigar, or pipe in it;

teeth, if drawn, that would have *moderate* line quality and would *not*
be drawn in a *very detailed, careful* fashion, *not jagged* or drawn as
one or a few spaced teeth.

Hair relates to an individual's *concern about his or her sexual attractiveness
or desirability. Optimally*, the drawn figure would have hair that would
involve:

moderate line quality and shading;

appropriate color—all except blue or green;

moderate extent (proportionate to the size of the head);

not being drawn in a *bizarre, disheveled, or messy* manner;

not having a *hat* unless it was appropriate to the figure.

☐ B. The TORSO

The torso includes the *neck, shoulders*, and *torso area*, which includes the
trunk, chest and *breasts, waist, midline, crotch area*, and *hips and buttocks*.

1) The Neck

The neck subjectively relates to the *conduit between cognitive activity*, e.g.,
thoughts, fantasies, affects, that occur in the mind (the head) and "mind-
less" *physical reactions* of the body (impulses). The inference is to a pas-
sageway—a mediating agency—where the proper integration or modulation results in a sense of *control of mind-body experience*. For example, the
expression, "having a thick neck," conveys the idea of stubbornness, i.e.,
minimal ability to flexibly adapt one's thoughts and actions; the expression, "sticking your neck out," implies taking a chance, i.e., relinquishing
control of your better judgment.

Omission

Where there is *no indication* of a neck, i.e., the head sits directly on the
shoulders or body and there is no suggestion of a neck area or a collar or
clothing within the body, the feeling evoked is of a *blunt, concrete, unreflec-
tive* orientation with regard to the integration or modulation of physical

FIGURE 6.10

behavior by cognitive activity with the implication of *lessened control* of the former (see Figure 6.10).

Where there is *no neck and the head is visibly separated from the body*, the sense is of a profound lack of control of physical reactions with the possibility of *dissociative behavior and/or a thought disorder*.

Size and Shape

An *overly long* neck, (i.e., disproportionately long relative to the size of the head and body), conveys a sense of the drawer's need to have *distance* between thoughts and actions, because of *anxiety* with regard to the possibility of impulsive behavior, i.e., of *insufficient self-control*. This implies the *inhibition* of the acting out of physical action with corresponding attitudes, feelings, and fantasies that stress control.

An *overly long-and-narrow* neck furthers the sense of *inhibition* to a point of *withdrawal and detachment* from situations where the potential for loss of control of behavior is greater.

An *overly wide* neck, (i.e., disproportionately wide relative to the size of the head and body), elicits a sense of *preoccupation* with issues of mind-body integration and control. The implication is of *inflexibility* and a *domineering* manner. The image of the thick-necked, overbearing sergeant comes to mind.

An *overly small* neck, (i.e., disproportionately short and/or narrow relative to the size of the head and body), conveys a sense of someone who has an *awareness* of control issues but feels *overwhelmed* by the experience of integrating mind and body. The feeling is of a person who has less ability to employ cognitive means to control behavior but who may adopt an overly *passive or inhibited* stance in order to achieve control.

An *overly short-and-wide* neck conveys the sense of someone who *may not be able to control impulsive behavior* either by cognitive activity or behavioral constriction.

When the neck is drawn as a *single line*, the sense is of a person who feels very *inadequate* to successfully control his physical impulses.

Connection of Neck to Head and Body

When the neck is *connected to the head but disconnected from the body*, the sense is of the presence of cognitive activity which is *inadequate* to control behavior.

When the neck is *attached to the body but disconnected from the head*, the sense is of the *unavailability of cognitive resources*, e.g., attitudes or fantasies, which could be utilized to control impulsive behavior.

Depending on how extreme these separations are, the possibility of a *thought disorder* exists.

Where a neck is present but there is *no neckline or collarline of a garment* on the body, the sense is of someone who experiences the presence of *bodily impulses flowing unimpeded* into the mind (see Figure 6.11).

2) Shoulders

FIGURE 6.11

Shoulders refer, subjectively, to the capacity to bear weight. The connotation relates to the ability to take on *responsibility*. The expression, "shouldering responsibility," bears directly on the inner process that underlies the drawing of this feature.

Omission

Not drawing shoulders on the male or female figure drawn front view or partly angled, i.e., with the torso extending directly from the head and the arms from the torso, conveys a sense of *extreme avoidance* with respect to one's capacity for

FIGURE 6.12

responsibility with the implication of *severe feelings of inadequacy*. The possibility is raised of an underlying *neurological disorder or mental retardation* (see Figure 6.12).

Size and Shape

Overly large shoulders, (i.e., disproportionately wide relative to the size of the body), elicit a sense of the drawer's need to *overcompensate for felt inadequacy* with respect to the ability to assume responsibility. The feeling evoked is of someone who attempts to *dominate* situations or *assume excessive authority*.

Overly small shoulders, (i.e., disproportionately narrow relative to the size of the body), convey a sense of the individual's conscious awareness of inadequacy with a tendency to *withdraw* from situations involving the need to assume responsibility and to adopt a *passive* stance.

Sharply squared shoulders evoke a sense of the person adopting a *rigid*, unwavering position in situations involving the need for responsible action.

Drooping shoulders elicit *depressive* feelings with regard to taking on the "burdens" of responsibility.

Unequal size shoulders convey feelings of *ambivalence*, i.e., one part of the

FIGURE 6.13

individual feels *capable* of assuming responsibility while one part feels *inadequate* to the task.

3) The Trunk

The *area between the collar bone and the crotch* is analogous to the trunk of the TREE in the sense that it relates, subjectively, to the part of the body from which one's feelings of *essential strength* emanate, i.e., of how capable or adequate one experiences oneself in terms of having the "inner stuff" to function in the world.

Omission

Not drawing a trunk, i.e., having the limbs come directly from the head, conveys a sense of *severe regression*—of having no sense of one's inner strength—with the possibility of a *thinking or neurological disorder or mental retardation* (see Figure 6.13).

Size and Shape

An *overly long* trunk, (i.e., disproportionately long relative to the overall size of the body), conveys a sense of *overcompensation for a felt lack of inner strength* by "extending oneself too thin," i.e., being *overactive* in terms of functioning.

An *overly wide* trunk, (i.e., disproportionately wide relative to the overall size of the body), elicits the feeling that the individual *overcompensates for feelings of inadequate strength* by "taking up a lot of space," i.e., adopting a *demanding or authoritarian* position.

An *overly small* trunk, (i.e., disproportionately short and/or narrow relative to the overall size of the body), elicits a sense of the drawer's felt experience of *inadequacy* with *passive and inhibited* behavioral consequences.

A trunk that is *overly long and narrow* conveys a sense of *felt -inadequacy* leading to *withdrawal* from interaction with others.

An *overly short and wide* trunk evokes a feeling of someone whose sense of his being in the world is like a "bull terrier," i.e., *small but ferocious if provoked*.

The *different areas of the trunk* subjectively relate to variations of the theme of inner strength associated with the trunk.

3a) The Chest

Generally, this feature would be considered for drawings of the *male* figure. If the trunk evokes the more general sense of strength, the chest appears to evoke a more specific sense of *power.* The subjective inferences will vary according to the *gender* of the drawer and to whether the focus of the experience is the *self* or a significant *selfobject.*

Size

Here, the feelings evoked are similar to those for the trunk as a whole, e.g., an *overly wide* chest conveys the feeling of someone *overcompensating for a felt lack of power* by adopting a "he-man" (*domineering*) stance.

An *overly narrow* chest conveys feelings of *felt inadequacy* accompanied by *passive and submissive* behavior.

If the chest of the male figure is drawn *bare,* the sense is of an *exhibitionistic overcompensation* for felt powerlessness. If drawn by a *male,* this could refer to the *self or a selfobject;* if drawn by a *female,* to the *latter.*

3b) Breasts

Generally, this feature would be considered for drawings of the *female* figure. Breasts connote both a source of *dependency, gratification, and sexual capacity and attractiveness.* Theoretically, if basic selfobject needs upon which the infant is dependent, e.g., nurturance, support, affirmation, are not provided, the ensuing state of felt abandonment and disintegration anxiety will lead to the emergence of sexual and aggressive drive derivatives. Thus, the manner in which breasts are dealt with by the drawer can provide considerable insight into his or her relative degree of maturity with regard to this fundamental self-selfobject involvement.

Omission

Not drawing breasts on the adult female figure by either a male or female drawer implies fundamental feelings of *frustration of dependency* needs. (If the *female is drawn as a child,* the implication is of *avoidance* of this felt experience.) For the drawing of an adult female, not drawing breasts by a *male* conveys a stronger sense of *denial* with regard to dependency need-gratification and the perception of the female selfobject as a sexually immature figure. For the *female* drawer, the self-experience would involve *felt inadequacy* as a nurturant or sexually mature figure and/or experiencing the female selfobject in this way.

Size

Overly large breasts, (i.e., disproportionately large relative to the size of the body), evoke a sense of *overcompensation for anxiety* with regard to dependency gratification with subsequent *over involvement* with sexual capacity and attractiveness.

If drawn by a *male*, the feelings evoked revolve around a *preoccupation* with the female selfobject's capacity to nourish. If drawn in a *sexually provocative* manner, overly large breasts then suggest *compensating* for unmet dependency needs by *overexaggerating or overidealizing* the female's sexual prowess and desirability with the possibility of voyeuristic behavior.

If drawn by a *female*, similar interpretations may be made with regard to dependency gratification by the female selfobject with the addition of a *self-identification as inadequate* both as a source of dependency gratification and in terms of sexual capability or desirability resulting in *exhibitionistic compensation*.

Overly small breasts, (i.e., disproportionately small relative to the the size of the body), elicit a sense of *inadequacy* of the female depicted as a provider of dependency gratification or as a source of sexual power or attractiveness.

If drawn by a *male*, the sense is of a *belittling or disparaging* attitude toward the female selfobject.

If drawn by a *female*, these same attitudes toward the female selfobject may be found, as well as a sense of *inferiority* as a female and, possibly, *sexual identity* problems.

Bare Breasts

When breasts are drawn of the *female* figure with *no indication of any clothing or covering*, if drawn by a *male*, the feeling evoked is of *voyeurism;* if drawn by a *female*, it is of *exhibitionism*. In both cases, there is a sense of *nonconformity, immaturity, and oppositionalism*.

When *breasts or breast-like protuberances are drawn on the male* figure, clothed or unclothed, the sense is of the male selfobject becoming the main source of dependency, gratification, and possibly sexual prowess. If drawn by either gender, the feeling is of a *distorted, regressed* sense of selfobject need gratification. For the *male* drawer, the element of *gender identity confusion* is added.

3c) The Waist

The area around the middle of the torso has subjective significance in the sense that the individual may feel that this is the dividing line between the upper region of the body and the lower or *sexual* area. The expression, "putting another notch on your belt," is a direct colloquial reference to making a sexual conquest. "Pulling in your belt," conveys a sense of coping with deprivation by "toughing" it out, i.e., exercising control and restraint. The self-experience for the drawer thus may be summarized as having to do with *containing or controlling sexual behavior*.

Omission

Often, male and female figures are drawn with no indication of special attention being paid to the waist. Figures of both sexes who are drawn wearing jackets that end below the waist or female figures wearing a dress are examples of this. However, where there is no indication of a dividing line, (usually a *belt*), of an unjacketed male or female figure wearing pants, the sense is of *avoidance* of the need to contain or control sexual behavior.

Size and Detailing of Waist Divider

An *overly large* divider, (i.e., disproportionately large relative to the size of the body), conveys the feeling of someone who *overcompensates for anxiety* related to the containing or control of sexual action by *excessively restrictive* control measures. If the divider is also *elaborately detailed*, the sense is of the person being *compulsive* in this effort.

An *overly small* divider, (i.e., disproportionately small relative to the size of the body), elicits the sense of someone who feels *overwhelmed and inadequate* to the task of containing and controlling sexual behavior.

3d) The Midline

Often, the figure is drawn with something drawing attention to the area going down the middle of the trunk. This may be represented as the *edge of an article of clothing*, a *line of buttons*, or a *hanging article such as a necktie or necklace*. The *omission* of such a midline representation appears to have *no special significance*. The *inclusion* may modify the basic sense of *power or strength* that the chest and trunk subjectively connote.

Buttons

Buttons have the connotation of securing a garment, holding it in place. Developmentally, the child requires assistance to fasten her buttons. Subjectively, then, buttons may refer to the need for selfobject assistance in order to present oneself in the world, a time when one's sense of inner strength was limited and one was *dependent upon others to achieve security*.

Size, Number, and Shape

Overly large and/or an excessive number of buttons, (i.e., disproportionately too big and/or too many for the type of garment), convey a sense of *preoccupation* with the need to achieve security. The implication is of a *dependent* orientation with the need to call attention to oneself or being *compulsively* driven to achieve the needed selfobject connection.

Buttons that are *elaborate* in shape also convey a sense of *exhibitionistic* behavior in the pursuit of securing dependency needs.

Overly small and/or too limited a number of buttons, (i.e., disproportionately too little and or too few for the type of garment), elicit a sense of *felt deprivation and passivity* with regard to achieving the needed dependency gratification.

Vertical Line or Hanging Article

A vertical line such as the edge of a jacket or shirt, when drawn, calls attention to the area of the body associated with the subjective sense of *inner strength or power*. Variations in *line quality and shading,* more so than *size,* are more frequently encountered in conveying the sense of *anxiety, tension, or uncertainty* with regard to the individual's self-experience of inner capability.

A *male* figure drawn with a necktie that hangs down the center of the chest focuses on a need to reinforce one's sense of capability with an article that connotes *formality and respectability.*

An *overly large* and/or *elaborate* tie conveys a sense of *overcompensation for felt inadequacy* by adopting an *overly imposing* stance.

An *overly small* tie elicits a sense of the drawer's experience of himself (or the significant selfobject) as *inadequate but making a feeble or half-hearted attempt to appear substantial.*

Female figures (and occasionally male figures) drawn with an *article of clothing or jewelry* hanging down the middle of the chest elicit feelings related to the attempt to *compensate for felt inadequacy* by diverting attention to an object of attractiveness.

3e) The Crotch Area

For *clothed* figures this includes the *fly area and/or the top inner leg lines* (if differentiated from the *whole* inner leg lines), if the figure is drawn with *pants or shorts*; or the area where the legs would join if the figure is wearing a *dress, skirt, or long garment*. If the figure is unclothed, it includes the *genitals* (see Figure 6.14).

FIGURE 6.14

The subjective experience related to the drawing of this feature seems to bear directly on the sense of *sexual adequacy.*

Omission

When the crotch area is blank, e.g., the figure is wearing a long garment, there may be no self-reference to sexual adequacy reflected in the drawing. However, if the *legs* are drawn *going straight up into the trunk without a definable crotch*, the sense is of *severe anxiety* leading to *avoidance and inhibition* of sexual activity (see Figure 6.15).

Similar to the *vertical line* drawn as the edge of a jacket or shirt, variations in *line quality and shading* of the *fly of the pants* or the *area where the legs join* in clothed figures are more frequent than variations in *size* in conveying the sense of *anxiety, tension, or uncertainty* with regard to feelings about sexual adequacy. *Anxiety* is also inferred when the *leg lines of a panted figure do not connect at the crotch*.

FIGURE 6.15

Genitals

Ordinarily, genitals are not shown. When they are, the sense is of someone experiencing *severe anxiety* with regard to their own or that of a significant selfobject's sense of sexual capability. These feelings may relate to the drawer's *insecurity about gender identity*. When genitals are drawn for the *same gender as the drawer*, the *compensatory* reaction relates to *exhibitionistic* tendencies; when shown for the *opposite gender*, the sense is of *voyeuristic* ones.

Size

Overly large genitals, (i.e., disproportionately large relative to the size of the body), in addition to the above, elicit a sense of the drawer's possible *inability to exert behavioral controls*.

Overly small genitals, (i.e., disproportionately small relative to the size of the body), add the dimension of *felt inadequacy* accompanied by *overly inhibited behavioral* tendencies.

3f) Hips and Buttocks

Mostly, this area of the torso is not drawn in such a way as to differentiate it from the outer leg or garment lines or area. If the figure is presented as front view or slightly angled, the hip area is seen. When the figure is shown in profile or rear view, the buttocks will be visible. When either part is distinguished, e.g., by *line quality or size*, the subjective connotation appears to involve feelings about *gender identity* related either to the self or a significant selfobject.

Size

Overly large hips or buttocks, (i.e., disproportionately large related to the size of the body), *drawn by a male of the male figure* convey a sense of *uncertainty or confusion* about one's own (or the male selfobject's) gender identity. If *drawn by a male of the female figure*, it may reflect an *overcompensation for anxiety* with regard to whether the female selfobject is experienced as capable of providing the gratification associated with that figure.

If *drawn by a female of the male figure*, it may represent a *displacement* of the feelings associated with the *maternal selfobject onto the male*. If *drawn by the female of the female figure*, it may reflect an overcompensation for anxiety with regard to the one's own gender identity or that of the female selfobject.

Overly small hips or buttocks, (i.e., disproportionately small relative to the size of the body), convey a feeling of *weakness and inadequacy* with regard to the sense of maleness or femaleness related to the self or the selfobject, regardless of the gender of the drawer or the figure drawn.

Bare Buttocks

In the unusual circumstance that buttocks are drawn without covering, either in profile or full rear view, the sense is of a disregard of usual convention. Colloquially, the act of "mooning," i.e., exhibiting one's bare bottom, implies *defiance and disdain*. Drawing a naked figure in such a way as to show the buttocks, elicits then a sense of *immaturity, oppositionalism, voyeurism*, and *exhibitionism* underscored by anxiety about one's own or the selfobject's gender identity.

Optimal Expressiveness with Regard to the Torso

The various subjective connotations associated with the different parts of the torso may be considered to be *optimally* reflected if *all* of the following conditions have been met for *both* the achromatic and chromatic drawings.

With regard to the *neck*, the feeling evoked relates to the drawer's sense of *control of mind-body experience*. An *optimal* presentation of the neck would involve:

> *moderate* line quality and shading;
> *color(s)* used for shading of skin are *appropriate*—black, brown, yellow, orange, red, not blue, green, or purple; (*any color used for clothing is appropriate*);
> *moderate* size and shape (proportionate to the size and shape of the body);
> *connection of the neck to the head and body.*

The *shoulders* refer, subjectively, to the ability to take on *responsibility.* An *optimal* expression would involve:

> *moderate* line quality and shading;
> *moderate* size and shape (proportionate to the size and shape of the body);
> *shoulders drawn clothed, not bare; (any color used for clothing is appropriate).*

The *trunk* relates feelings of *inner strength. Optimally,* the drawing would involve:

> *moderate* line quality and shading;
> *moderate* size and shape (proportionate to the size and shape of the body);
> trunk drawn *clothed, not bare; (any color used for clothing is appropriate).*

The *chest of the male* figure evokes the feeling of *power. Optimally,* the drawing would involve:

> *moderate* line quality and shading;
> *moderate* size and shape (proportionate to the size and shape of the body);
> chest drawn *clothed, not bare; (any color used for clothing is appropriate).*

Breasts connote both a source of *dependency, gratification, and sexual capacity and attractiveness.* An *optimal* presentation would involve:

> *moderate* line quality and shading;
> *moderate* size and shape (proportionate to the size and shape of the body);
> breasts drawn *clothed, not bare; (any color used for clothing is appropriate;* breasts *not drawn on the male figure.*

The *waist* involves the subjective sense of *containing or controlling sexual behavior.* If a *waist divider* is drawn, *optimally,* its presentation would involve:

> *moderate* line quality and shading;
> *moderate* size (proportionate to the size of the body) and detailing;
> *any color* used for waist divider is *appropriate.*

A *midline* representation relates to *variations of the basic sense of power* or strength. Presented as *buttons,* the subjective connotation refers to *dependency upon others to achieve security.* As a *vertical line or hanging article,* it conveys *modifications of the sense of adequacy. Optimally,* the various presentations would include the following:

all have *moderate* line quality and shading;
buttons have *moderate* size, number, and shape;
ties (and other hanging articles) have *moderate* size and detailing;
any color used for midline representation is appropriate.

The *crotch area* relates, subjectively, to the sense of *sexual adequacy*. An optimal representation would involve:

moderate line quality and shading;
connection of leg lines of a panted figure;
area is *clothed (genitals are not exposed);*
any color used for clothing is appropriate.

Hips and buttocks refer to one's sense of *gender identity*. *Optimally*, this would involve:

moderate line quality and shading;
moderate size (proportionate to the size of the body);
area is clothed (buttocks are not bare);
any color used for clothing is appropriate).

☐ C. The LIMBS

The limbs include the *arms, hands, legs, and feet (including shoes).*

1) The Arms

The arms include the area leaving the body to where the hands begin. They may be drawn bare or clothed. The arms relate, subjectively, to one's capacity to carry out intentions, to reach out and make contact with sources of selfobject gratification—in sum, to *connect with the environment.*

Omission

When either or both of the arms is omitted, the manner of its (their) omission is significant. When *one arm is clearly not drawn* in a full-face figure, the sense is of a *repressive* process, of something that is blocking the person from completing the act of connecting with the environment. The feeling is of inner conflict resulting in an *ambivalent* state, i.e., in part, the person is motivated to attempt connection and in part she represses the process.

If *both arms are not drawn*, the feeling evoked is more severe. The sense is one of *helplessness, vulnerability, felt inadequacy*. It suggests a *regressive* process relating the individual to *infantile status*. The feelings evoked also include a *crippled body image, depressiveness, withdrawal, and distorted reality perception.*

When *one arm is fully concealed* in a full-face figure, or the figure is drawn on an angle or in profile so that one arm cannot be seen, the sense is of a more conscious process of *evasiveness* as a response to the drawer's underlying *ambivalence* about connecting with the environment.

If *both arms are fully concealed,* (as with the arms held behind the back), the feeling is one of *severe evasiveness and constriction,* as if the person were holding something back from being observed and, in the process, severely constricting his ability to connect with the surround.

When *one arm is either incompletely drawn, partially concealed, or partially cut off by the edge of the page,* in addition to *evasiveness and ambivalence,* the feelings evoked include *constriction and inhibition of action.*

If *both arms* are treated in one of these ways, the sense is less of ambivalence and evasiveness and more of a *compelling urge to inhibit and constrict* one's ability to interconnect with the world.

Size and Shape

Overly long arms, (i.e., disproportionately long relative to the size of the body), convey a sense of *overcompensating for feelings of inadequacy* with regard to being able to connect with the environment by being *overactive,* i.e., extending oneself too far.

Overly wide arms, (i.e., disproportionately wide relative to the size of the body), elicit the feeling that the person *overcompensates for a felt inability* to make connections by being too *controlling or domineering.*

Arms (of *any* length or width) that are drawn with the *muscles clearly delineated* add the dimension of the drawer's emphasizing his (or the selfobject's) *strength* and subsequent ability to connect with the environment by an *assertive or aggressive* stance (depending on the expression and posture of the figure).

Overly short and/or thin arms, (i.e., disproportionately short and/or thin relative to the size of the body), elicit feelings of *inadequacy, inhibition, and passivity.* When the arms are also drawn as *wavery or ribbon-like,* the sense is of *severe passivity and felt inadequacy.* The possibility of a *neurological disorder* is raised.

Arms that are drawn as *single lines* convey feelings of *severe felt inadequacy* with regard to connecting with the environment.

Unequal size arms, (i.e., the length or width of the two arms is clearly dissimilar), convey feelings of *ambivalence* with regard to the ability to connect with the environment. This expression of a lack of a consistent attitude may underlie both *passive and aggressive* behavioral tendencies. *Extreme discrepancy* in the drawing of the two arms may indicate the presence of a *neurological disorder or mental retardation.*

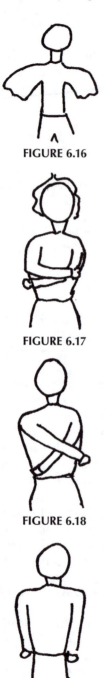

FIGURE 6.16

FIGURE 6.17

FIGURE 6.18

When the arms are drawn as *wing-like*, the feeling evoked is of *distorted reality perception* with the possibility of a *thinking or neurological disorder* (see Figure 6.16).

Position

Arms that are presented as *folded across the chest* convey a sense of *guardedness, suspiciousness, and hostility* with regard to the person's experience of interconnecting with the environment (see Figure 6.17).

When arms are drawn as *crossed across the body*, the feeling seems to be more one of *defending* oneself *by blocking off* interconnectedness (see Figure 6.18).

Arms drawn *tightly against the body* (no visible space between arm and body) elicit feelings of *rigidity and inhibition* (see Figure 6.19).

If arms are drawn as *contained within the body*, the sense is of *severe constriction* (see Figure 6.20).

Arms that are held *akimbo*, i.e., elbows out, hands on hips, convey an attitude of "don't mess with me," i.e., an *aggressive defensiveness* (see Figure 6.21).

Similarly, arms that are *held away from the body but curved toward the hips* elicit an *aggressive*, possibly *menacing* feeling (see Figure 6.22).

When arms are drawn as *fully outstretched*, the sense is of someone who is *over eager* for interconnectedness with others (see Figure 6.23).

Arms that are *fully detached from the trunk* convey a feeling of *severe anxiety* with regard to connecting with others; this suggests a *distortion of reality* with

FIGURE 6.19   **FIGURE 6.20**    **FIGURE 6.21**

the possibility of dissociated behavior (see Figure 6.24).

When the arms are drawn *extending from the trunk, not at the shoulder,* the sense is again of distortion, but here with the feeling that the individual has *serious perceptual problems,* suggesting the possibility of a *neurological disorder or mental retardation* (see Figure 6.25).

Similarly, but more severely, when the arms are drawn *extended from the head,* the impression is of a young child's drawing suggesting profound *regressiveness* with the possibility of a *neurological disorder or mental retardation* (see Figure 6.26).

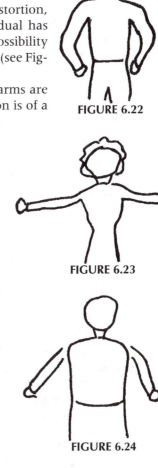

FIGURE 6.22

FIGURE 6.23

Transparency

When the arms are drawn so that they can be *seen through the clothing,* the subjective sense is of a *break with reality perception.* Depending on the severity or extent of the presentation, e.g., possibly the result of a hurried effort, this could indicate *narcissistic self-absorption* resulting in a *careless, thoughtless approach* to connecting with the environment all the way to the possibility of a *thinking disorder* (see Figure 6.27).

2) The Hands

Hands include the area at the end of the arms differentiated from the arm by an in-

FIGURE 6.24

FIGURE 6.25   FIGURE 6.26   FIGURE 6.27

dentation (the "wrist") or a line, e.g., sleeve cuff. The subjective connotation includes the fingers, outlined or implied.

Subjectively, hands are the refined extensions of the individual's ability to connect with the environment, to make contact with sources of selfobject need gratification. Hands enable the person to manipulate objects, to interact in a precise, detailed manner or in a gross, aggressive fashion. The sense conveyed by the drawing of hands, then, is of the *ability to control the environment*, to deal directly with the selfobject experience.

Omission

When *one hand* is clearly not drawn where *both arms* are shown, the feeling elicited (similar to the arms) is of a blocking of the thought process, of underlying *ambivalence* about actually assuming control. Since the arm has been drawn, the sense is of a desire to connect with the environment on the one hand, conflicting with *anxiety* about exerting control on the other.

When *both hands* are not drawn, the sense (as when both arms are not drawn) is of *severe felt inadequacy, a crippled body image, and distorted reality perception*. Again, since the arms have been drawn, the inner conflict revolves around a desire to connect versus a profound hesitancy to exert effective control.

If *one hand is fully concealed*, e.g., in a pocket or behind the back, or if the figure is drawn on an angle or in profile, the sense is of *evasiveness* with regard to exerting control.

If *both hands are fully concealed*, the feeling conveyed combines both *severe evasiveness* (as if the person has something to hide) and *constriction* (as if the person is preventing herself from performing some action).

When *one hand is either incompletely drawn, partially concealed, or partially cut off by the edge of the page*, the feelings evoked are those of *ambivalence, constriction, and inhibition*.

If *both hands are drawn in one of these ways*, the sense is of the drawer's more compelling *conflict* about controlling the environment with a greater degree of the above felt experiences.

FIGURE 6.28

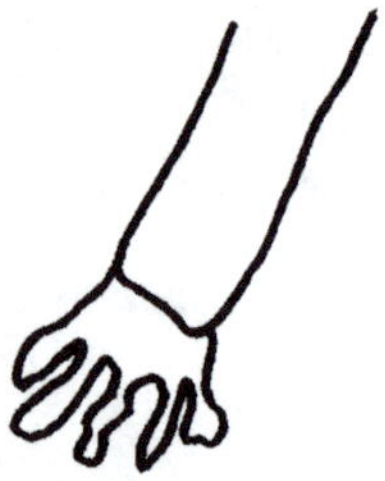

FIGURE 6.29

FIGURE 6.30

Size and Shape

Overly large hands, (i.e., disproportionately long and/ or wide relative to the size of the arms), convey a sense of *overcompensating for feelings of inadequacy* with regard to being able to control the environment by being *overactive or assertive*, i.e., trying to do too much.

Overly small hands, (i.e., disproportionately short and/or narrow relative to the size of the arms), convey the opposite feelings, i.e., someone who experiences himself as too *inadequate* to exert control and who behaves in a *passive, inhibited* manner.

FIGURE 6.31

When hands of any size are drawn in *profile*, (i.e., side view with [possibly] only the thumb outlined), the sense is of a person who *constricts* her efforts to control the surroundings.

Small hands with pointed fingers evoke a sense of someone who feels *inadequate* but acts in a *surreptitious, hostile* manner in order to exert control (see Figure 6.28).

FIGURE 6.32

Hands of any size that appear *weak looking*, i.e., floppy or wavery, convey a strong sense of *felt inadequacy* (see Figure 6.29).

When hands are drawn as a *circle or oval with no extended fingers*, again the sense is of feelings of *inadequacy and helplessness* (see Figure 6.30).

When *one-dimensional fingers (straight lines) are enclosed by a loop*, the feeling is of someone who is *suppressing or constricting* his efforts to achieve control (see Figure 6.31).

FIGURE 6.33

When the *straight lines protrude from the loop*, the subjective impression is like that of a child's drawing with the implication of *regressiveness* in attempting to control the field and aggressive, unmodulated behavior (see Figure 6.32).

If *only fingers are drawn with no palm area*, (i.e., fingers join directly with arm or sleeve), the feeling is similar and the sense is of a potential for *blunt* behavior (see Figure 6.33).

Moderate or large hands with spike-like fingers, (i.e., the ends are pointed or appear as sharp nails or claws), convey a strong feeling of *hostility and aggressive* behavior in attempting to achieve control (see Figure 6.34).

FIGURE 6.34

When hands are drawn as *fists,* (i.e., lines indicating clenched fingers or knuckles are drawn), the sense is of *anger and defiance* with regard to achieving control (see Figure 6.35).

When *gloves* are drawn covering the hands, the sense is of someone covering up feelings relating to control. The feeling is of a *muted, indirect* approach to interacting by presenting a more *refined* picture (see Figure 6.36).

FIGURE 6.35

Hands that are covered by *mittens* elicit a child-like feel, suggesting *regressiveness* and an *undifferentiated* way of interacting (see Figure 6.37).

Hands that are drawn with *petal-like fingers,* i.e., rounded or short and fat with rounded ends), *irregular contours,* or are *unequal in size,* all elicit a sense of *regressiveness, distortion, and lack of control* that are suggestive of a *neurological disorder* (see Figure 6.38).

FIGURE 6.36

Position

When hands are drawn *holding an object,* the sense is of an attempt to *compensate for anxiety* about achieving control. The interpretation is elaborated by the nature of the object held.

Hands that are drawn *covering the pelvic area,* (the "pelvic defense"), subjectively connote an attempt to *control sexual anxiety* (see Figure 6.39).

When the *hands are detached from the arms* or the *fingers are detached from the hands,* the sense is of a *distortion of reality* with the possibility of *dissociated* behavior.

FIGURE 6.37

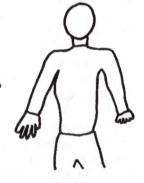

FIGURE 6.38

Fingers–Number and Additional Characteristics

Too few fingers, (i.e., *less than five* where fingers are outlined and the whole hand can be seen), elicit a sense of *felt inadequacy* with regard to achieving control.

Too many fingers, (i.e., *more than five* where fingers are outlined and the whole hand can be seen), convey a feeling of *excessive activity and overeagerness* in attempting to achieve control.

FIGURE 6.39

When fingers are shown with the *joints and fingernails overly carefully* drawn, the sense is of an *obsessive-compulsive compensation* for anxiety with regard to the issue of control.

3) The Legs

Legs include the area leaving the torso beneath the crotch to where the feet begin. They may be drawn bare or clothed. Legs relate subjectively to the person's capacity to make changes in his position for some desired end, e.g., to approach sources of gratification, escape from danger, or be able to support oneself. This may be summarized as one's *maneuverability* in the world.

Omission

When *one leg is clearly not drawn* in a full-face figure, as with the omission of *one arm*, the sense is of something *blocking* the thought process with regard to maneuvering in the world. The feeling is of a handicap, a crippling *ambivalence* that lessens one's capacity to function.

If *both legs are not drawn*, the feeling is of utter *helplessness and felt inadequacy*. The empathic sense is of *being crippled, half a person*. This evokes feelings of *depression and withdrawal*.

If *one leg is fully concealed*, e.g., by an object, or if the figure is drawn on an angle or in profile so that one leg cannot be seen, the feeling evoked is one of *evasiveness* as a response to an underlying *ambivalence* about maneuvering in the world.

If *both legs are fully concealed*, e.g., behind a desk, the sense is of *severe resistance* and *evasiveness* with regard to maneuvering.

When *one leg is either incompletely drawn, partially concealed, or partially cut off by an edge* (usually the bottom) *of the page*, the feeling is of *ambivalence* with resulting *constriction and inhibition* of action.

When *both legs are drawn in one of these ways*, the *severity* of these feelings is emphasized.

Size and Shape

Overly long legs, (i.e., disproportionately long relative to the size of the body), convey a sense of *overcompensation for feelings of inadequacy* with regard to being able to maneuver by being *overactive or overstriving*.

Overly wide legs, (i.e., disproportionately wide relative to the size of the body), elicit the sense of a person who *overcompensates* by occupying too much space in her attempt to maneuver, i.e., who may be too *controlling*.

Muscular legs (of any length or width) add the feeling of *assertiveness or aggressiveness* (depending on the expression and posture of the figure).

Overly short and/or thin legs, (i.e., disproportionately short and/or thin relative to the size of the body), convey the drawer's sense of *inadequacy, inhibition, and passivity* in attempting to maneuver in the world. *Wavery or ribbon-like* legs add the sense of *severe passivity and felt inadequacy* with the possibility of a *neurological disorder*.

Legs that are drawn as *single lines* elicit feelings of *severe felt inadequacy*.

Unequal-size legs, (i.e., the length or width of the two legs is clearly dissimilar), convey feelings of *ambivalence* with regard to maneuverability, suggesting both *passive and assertive or aggressive* tendencies. *Extreme discrepancy* may indicate the presence of a *neurological disorder or mental retardation*.

Position

Closed legs, (i.e., pressed together with a single line used to represent the demarcation of the two legs), give a sense of *rigidity*. The proximity to the crotch adds the suggestion of *sexual inhibition* (see Figure 6.40).

Crossed legs also convey a sense of *sexual anxiety and inhibition* (see Figure 6.41).

A *broad-based stance*, (i.e., legs spread wide apart), convey a feeling of *overcompensating for insecurity* with regard to maneuvering by adopting a *defiant* position (see Figure 6.42).

Legs that are *fully detached from the trunk* elicit a sense of *severe anxiety* with regard to maneuvering in the world. This *distortion of realistic perception* suggests the possibility of *dissociated* behavior (see Figure 6.43).

When legs are drawn at the very *base of the page*, (i.e., legs or skirt [not feet or shoes] touch or almost touch the bottom of the page), the sense is of strong feelings of *insecurity and cconstriction*.

FIGURE 6.40   **FIGURE 6.41**

Transparency

When the legs are drawn so that they can be *seen through the clothing*, the sense is of *distortion of reality perception*. As with the arms, this may indicate *narcissistic self-absorption* or a *severe reality break* suggestive of a *thinking disorder* (see Figure 6.44).

4) The Feet

The feet include the area at the end of the legs differentiated from the legs by an indentation (the "ankle") or a line, e.g., a pants cuff or the top of the shoe. They may be drawn bare or with shoes.

Subjectively, the feet, being in direct contact with the ground, represent the primary organ for positioning oneself in the world. Feet enable the person to balance herself, to move forward or backward. This capacity enables the individual to achieve the appropriate degree of *relative autonomy* vis-a-vis sources of selfobject need gratification. Self psychology posits that absolute independence from such experience does not represent an optimally mature state, in fact, it is impossible. The drawing of feet, then, connotes how, subjectively, the individual deals with finding his place along the continuum of dependence-independence with regard to the selfobject experience. The expressions, "standing on one's own two feet" and "putting one's foot down," convey the sense of relative autonomy and self-determination that the drawing of feet represent.

Omission

One foot not drawn where both legs are shown (as with the omission of the hands) conveys the feeling of a blocking of perception suggesting *ambivalence* about being autonomous.

When *both feet are not drawn*, the sense is of *severe felt inadequacy* with regard to standing relatively independent in the world along with *distortions of body image and reality perception*. Since the legs are drawn, the drawer is dealing with the issue of

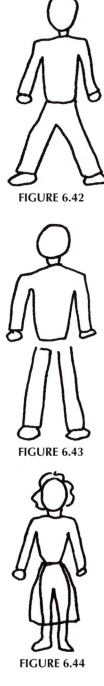

FIGURE 6.42

FIGURE 6.43

FIGURE 6.44

maneuvering in the world but not with the need to take a relatively autonomous stance in it.

When *one foot is fully concealed*, e.g., by an object, or the figure is drawn on an angle or in profile, the feeling is that the drawer is being *evasive* about the issue of autonomy.

If *both feet are fully concealed*, the feeling evoked (as with the hands) combines *severe evasiveness with constriction*.

When *one foot is either incompletely drawn, partially concealed, or partially cut off by an edge of the page*, the sense is of *ambivalence, constriction, and inhibition* with respect to taking a relatively autonomous stance.

When *both feet are drawn in one of these ways*, the feeling is of a more *extreme* sense of *ambivalence* with commensurate limitations in the ability to stand on one's own two feet.

Size and Shape

Overly large feet, (i.e., disproportionately long and/or wide relative to the size of the legs), elicit feelings of *overcompensating for feelings of inadequacy* with regard to being autonomous by *overstressing one's independence*.

Overly small feet, (i.e., disproportionately short and/or narrow relative to the size of the legs), convey a sense of *felt inadequacy* with regard to autonomy with consequent *fearfulness and passivity*.

When feet or shoes are drawn as *round or oval shapes with no details*, e.g., laces or heels, the sense is of *child-like immaturity and restricted* autonomy (see Figure 6.45).

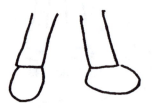

FIGURE 6.45

Sharply-pointed feet or shoes, (i.e., tip or heel), convey a sense of *hostile-aggressiveness* with regard to achieving autonomy. If toes are separately drawn in this manner, the sense is of a *primitive regressiveness* (see Figure 6.46).

"Chicken feet," (i.e., multiple straight lines or curved, talon-like ones), convey a sense of *severely distorted reality perception* with the

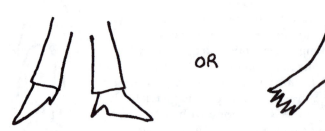

FIGURE 6.46

possibility of a *thinking or neurological disorder or mental retardation* (see Figure 6.47).

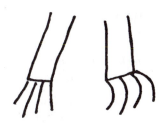

FIGURE 6.47

Position

Standing on tiptoe elicits a feeling of *hypercautiousness* with regard to standing on one's own feet.

Feet that are *markedly pointing in opposite directions* convey a sense of *indecisiveness*.

Feet that are *fully detached from the legs* convey feelings of *severe anxiety* in achieving autonomy. The implication is of *reality distortion* with the possibility of *dissociated* behavior.

Feet that are drawn as *touching (or almost touching) the base of the page* convey feelings of *inadequacy and insecurity* with the concurrent *need for support*.

Detailing

Overly detailed or elaborate shoes, e.g., laces, wing tips, bows or other details, are either *excessively or too carefully* drawn, conveying a sense of *obsessive-compulsive* preoccupation with the issue of autonomy. *Compensatory exhibitionism for felt inadequacy* may also be indicated. *Boots* convey a sense of the drawer needing to present something greater than ordinary shoes suggesting a need for *reinforcement or protection* in achieving relative autonomy. If the figure is presented, for example, as a cowboy or a fisherman, the drawing of boots appropriate to that figure might have another connotation.

Bare Feet

Where the figure is *clothed and feet are drawn as bare*, the feeling conveyed is of an *exhibitionistic, nonconformist* person who may manifest *oppositional* behavior in the environment.

Optimal Expressiveness with Regard to the Limbs

The empathically derived interpretations associated with the arms and hands and of the legs and feet of the male and female figures have been described separately because each unit had a unique connotation. However, for the purpose of considering what is an optimal representation in the drawings, nothing about the arms can be considered optimal if the hands are not drawn, and, similarly, the legs cannot be thought of as *optimally* presented if the feet are not included. So, assuming that the limbs have been drawn intact, they may be considered to be *optimally* represented if *all* of the following conditions have been met for *both* the achromatic and chromatic drawings.

With regard to the *arms*, the sense conveyed relates to the individual's *ability to connect* with sources of selfobject gratification. An *optimal* presentation of the arms would include:

> *moderate* line quality and shading;
> *color(s)* used for shading of skin are *appropriate*: black, brown, yellow, orange, red, not blue, green, or purple; (any color used for clothing is appropriate;
> *both arms fully revealed);*
> *moderate* size and shape (proportionate to the size and shape of the body);
> *connection of the arms to the body at the shoulders;*
> *arms* held in a *relaxed and flexible position;*
> *arms cannot be seen through clothing.*

The *hands* subjectively connote the person's ability to effectively manipulate or *control* environmental sources of selfobject gratification. *Optimally*, the drawing would involve:

> *moderate* line quality and shading;
> *color(s)* used for shading of skin are *appropriate*: black, brown, yellow, orange, red, not, blue, green, or purple;
> *moderate* size and shape of hands and fingers (proportionate to size and shape of arms);
> *hands not drawn in profile, as fists, or wearing gloves or mittens;*
> *hands held in a relaxed and flexible manner, not holding an object and not covering the pelvic area;*
> *hands connected to arms and fingers connected to hands;*
> *hands have five fingers* which do *not have joints and fingernails overly carefully drawn.*

The *legs* evoke the feeling of being able to *maneuver* in order to obtain selfobject gratification. An *optimal* presentation would involve:

> *moderate* line quality and shading;
> *color(s)* used for shading of skin are *appropriate*: black, brown, yellow, orange, red, not blue, green, or purple; (any color used for clothing is *appropriate);*
> *both legs fully revealed;*
> *moderate* size and shape (proportionate to size and shape of body);
> *legs connected to body and are relatively straight and slightly apart if figure is standing; appropriately angled if figure is moving;*
> *legs do not touch bottom of page;*
> *legs cannot be seen through clothing.*

The *feet* relate, subjectively, to one's sense of *relative autonomy*. *Optimally,* the drawing would involve:

> *moderate* line quality and shading;
>
> *color(s)* used for shading of skin are *appropriate*: black, brown, yellow, orange, red, not blue, green, or purple; (any color used for shoes is appropriate);
>
> *moderate size and shape of feet or shoes* (proportionate to size and shape of legs);
>
> *feet connected to legs and relatively straight or slightly angled, not on tiptoe or markedly pointing in opposite directions;*
>
> *shoes are not overly detailed or elaborated;*
>
> *boots are not drawn unless connected to an appropriate figure;*
>
> *feet are not bare in a fully clothed figure;*
>
> *feet or shoes do not touch base of page.*

☐ D. The WHOLE PERSON

The initial impressionistic analysis of the male and female figures is meant to provide the therapist with an opportunity to respond to the subjective experience of the drawer on a broad, global level in terms of what is revealed about self-structure. Here, we will explore how various presentations of the structure and type of the *whole figure* relate to specific, relevant aspects with regard to the dimensions of self-experience or that of the source of selfobject experiences.

1) Body Configuration

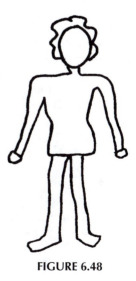

Subjectively, the manner in which the drawer configures the whole person with regard to the balance of the different parts relates to the sense of inner harmony, to one's feeling of being held together in a coordinated way, i.e., to the sense of *self-cohesion* with reference to the cognitive, affective, and behavioral elements that comprise the individual's experience-in-the-world.

When the figure appears to be *out-of-balance*, (i.e., the head, torso, and limbs are not in proper proportion to each other), the sense is of a *lack of feelings of self-cohesiveness* with *compensatory and defensive* structures focused on those features that are exaggerated (see Figure 6.48).

FIGURE 6.48

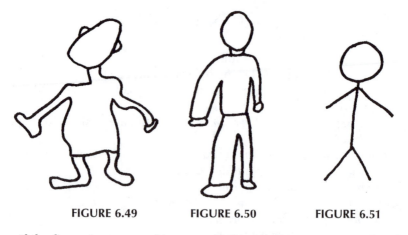

FIGURE 6.49	FIGURE 6.50	FIGURE 6.51

If the figure is presented in a *grossly disproportionate* manner, (i.e., in an exaggerated fashion, it does not conform to basic human proportions with regard to the size and shape of its parts), the feeling conveyed is one of *severely disturbed reality perception* with reference to the sense of self-cohesion. The possibility of a *thinking or neurological disorder* is raised (see Figure 6.49).

When the figure is drawn in an *asymmetrical* manner, (i.e., one side is extremely disproportionate in size or different in shape from the other side), the sense is of a *split* in the drawer's felt inner cohesion with the possibility of *dissociated* behavior (see Figure 6.50).

2) Body Authenticity

The way the person presents the drawn body in terms of its conformity to average, acceptable physical dimensions is a significant component in how he experiences his (or the selfobject's) authenticity or actual being-in-the-world. This can be summarized as the sense of *self-realization*.

The instructions request the drawer to draw a "whole person, not a stick figure." If the respondent does then draw a *stick figure*, (i.e., round head and only single lines for trunk and limbs), the feeling evoked is one of *oppositionalism and evasiveness* underscored by *strong feelings of inadequacy and insecurity* with a *diminished* sense of self-realization. The possibility of a *neurological disorder or mental retardation* should be considered (see Figure 6.51).

When the figure is presented as a *blank outline*, (i.e., a whole figure is presented but with no inner features), the sense is of *severe evasion and withdrawal* from interacting with the world; the impression is of a ghost-like presence. The absence of an awareness of one's inner resources points to *severely diminished* self-realization with a sense of *emptiness* that accompanies a *depressive* disorder (see Figure 6.52).

In a similar vein, a figure that is drawn in a *primitive* fashion, (i.e., simple, barely differentiated shapes for the various body parts and minimal details), gives a sense of an *undeveloped* self, functioning on a *regressive* level. A *thinking or neurological disorder or mental retardation* should be considered (see Figure 6.53).

A *geometric* figure, (i.e., squares, circles, etc. are used for body parts), amplifies the feeling of *impaired reality perception and a severe disturbance* in the sense of one's authentic presence in the world. Again, the possibility of a *neurological disorder or mental retardation* is raised (see Figure 6.54).

A *bizarre, grotesque, or dehumanized* figure, (i.e., the figure is drawn with weird, monstrous, or nonhuman features), elicits feelings of a *profound disturbance* in one's sense of being real and points to a *thinking or neurological disorder*.

3) Body Image

The *kind* of person that the drawer presents, i.e., how similar to or different from an average adult dressed in customary fashion the drawn figure is, conveys a sense of how one personifies oneself, who one experiences oneself to be—one's sense of *self-identity*.

When the *gender* of the figure *cannot be determined* from the drawing, the feeling elicited is one of *ambivalence or confusion* regarding the drawer's *gender identity* (see Figure 6.55).

If an adult draws a figure that appears like or is identified as a *child*, the feeling is that the drawer experiences herself (or the relevant selfobject) in a *nonthreatening* but *less autonomous, less-than-capable* manner. If the figure is drawn as a *baby*, these feelings are magnified.

A figure that appears *extremely thin, puny, or emaciated* elicits a sense of the drawer's identity reflecting feelings of *powerlessness* with a strong propensity for *depression*.

A figure that appears *obese or grossly overweight* evokes the feeling that the drawer's sense of identity reflects *self-contempt*, again with *depressive* affect.

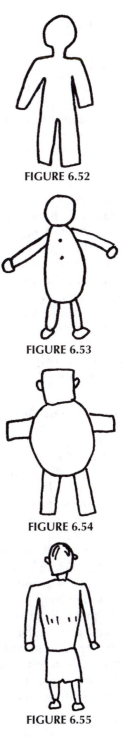

FIGURE 6.52

FIGURE 6.53

FIGURE 6.54

FIGURE 6.55

Figures that are drawn *totally nude* evoke the sense of *exhibitionistic over-compensation* for feelings of *inadequacy and insecurity* with reference to gender identity.

If the figure has a *seductive pose, clothed or unclothed,* the emphasis appears to be on experiencing oneself (or the selfobject) as using *sexually manipulative behavior* to shore up one's sense of identity.

An *occult* figure, e.g., a *ghost,* elicits a sense of the drawer having a *disturbed reality orientation* with regard to his self-identity with a tendency to *withdraw* from active relational participation.

Witches or vampires share the sense of *disturbance in reality orientation,* but convey feelings of *hostility* with regard to interpersonal involvement.

Religious figures such as *saints* also point to feelings of *unreality* with regard to self-identity with implications for *idealization of a passive, non-aggressive, nonsexual* behavioral style.

On the other hand, presenting the figure in a *silly* manner such as a *clown or cartoon* elicits feelings of *felt inferiority and low self-esteem.* The implication is for *regressive, impulsive* behavior.

Cartoons or caricatures of known figures convey a sense of *evasion and oppositionalism* with regard to revealing one's real identity.

Stereotyped figures, e.g., a *policeman,* a *cowboy,* also elicit feelings of *evasiveness* with regard to self-revelation. The sense is of the drawer attempting to *distance* herself from a direct expressiveness in terms of aspects of one's identity that the figure selected may nevertheless reveal.

Clothing and Additional Objects

The *manner* in which the figure is *clothed,* and whether it is drawn with something added to it, or held by it, also relate to how the person conveys a meaningful message with regard to self-identity.

When the figure is *elaborately dressed or overdressed,* the subjective connotation is of an *overcompensation for uncertainty* about who one is. The sense is of one attempting to mask this *anxiety* by drawing attention to the surface, i.e., by *exhibitionistic* behavior.

Similarly, an *underdressed* figure, i.e., the figure is wearing one or more articles of clothing without being full clothed, e.g., a *bathing suit,* elicits a feeling of *compensatory exhibitionism* to deal with underlying anxiety about one's identity.

Where individual garments have *excessive or repetitious detailing,* the sense is of *compensatory compulsive* behavior to deal with *anxiety* about self-identity.

In the discussion of the *hands, holding an object* was seen as *compensating for anxiety* about attaining control, about achieving gratification for selfobject needs in the environment. The *nature of the object* is relevant to the way this is manifested.

When the figure is *holding an object* such as a *purse, briefcase*, or *package, anxiety* about self-identity leads to *displacement* of selfobject needs and is *compensated* for by *dependence* on an external object.

The *holding of sports equipment or tools* suggests that the *compensatory structures* involve *action or a flight into activity*; the *holding of weapons* points to *aggressive compensatory structures*.

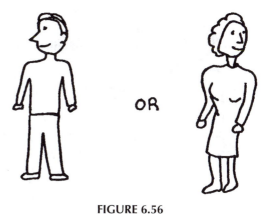

FIGURE 6.56

Objects drawn apart from the figure, i.e., a *car, building*, or *tree*, evoke a feeling of the person more *actively* involving the selfobject milieu in order to shore up his sense of identity.

Position

How the figure is depicted as holding itself relates subjectively to the sense of who one is, what qualities or defects comprise one's self-identity.

Active, noninterpersonally violent movement or stance, e.g., *chopping wood*, convey a sense of identity that implies an *assertive* orientation.

Interpersonally violent movement, e.g., *fighting, shooting*, subjectively connotes *aggressiveness*. The *degree* to which these activities are *socially channeled*, e.g., *a boxing match versus a fist fight*, suggests the *degree of behavioral control* and *extent of hostility* that the drawer experiences with regard to feelings about the kind of person she is.

When the figure is drawn in a *mixed* position, e.g., profile head on a front-body figure or the face turned one way, the body another, elicits a sense of *ambivalence* about one's identity (see Figure 6.56).

A figure that is *slanting or leaning*, i.e., an upright figure noticeably *tilted* to the side, conveys a sense of *uncertainty and insecurity* about one's identity.

A *floating* figure, i.e., the feet and legs are slanted and appear to be above the ground, exacerbate these feelings to the point where one's sense of identity is so *uncertain* as to promote a feeling of *detachment* from the self (see Figure 6.57).

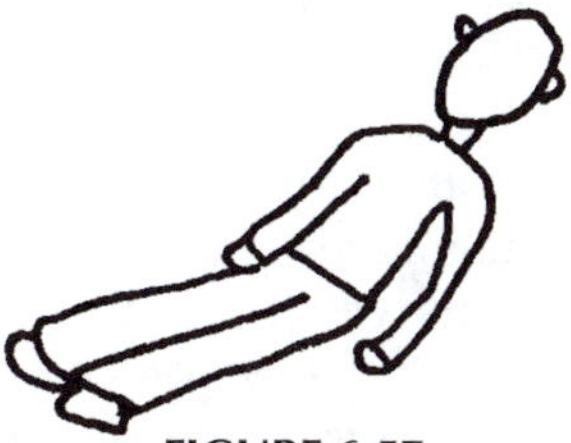

A *seated, lying down, or reclining* figure evokes a sense of *passivity* as a strong element in one's sense of identity.

FIGURE 6.57

If the figure is in a relatively *inert, immobile* position, the feeling is one of *passivity, inhibition, and affective constriction* (see Figure 6.58).

4) Relationship of MALE and FEMALE Drawings

In terms of the comparison of the MALE and FEMALE drawings, the *order of drawings*, the *relative height of the figures*, and the *sexual appearance* of the figures relate, subjectively, to the drawer's feelings about his or her own and the source of selfobject gratification's *gender identity*.

Order of Drawings and Height of Figures

FIGURE 6.58

When the MALE figure is drawn first.   If drawn by a *male* and the MALE figure is *considerably taller* than the FEMALE, the sense is of the drawer's *uncertainty* about his gender identity with feelings of *superiority* with regard to the female enjoined to *overcompensate for this anxiety*; if the MALE figure is *shorter* than the FEMALE, feelings of *ambivalence and inferiority* about gender identity are conveyed and the tendency is to *overidealize* the female selfobject.

If drawn by a *female* and the MALE figure is *considerably taller* than the FEMALE figure, the sense is of the drawer's *anxiety* about her gender identity with feelings of *inferiority, inadequacy, and a passive-submissive* orientation toward the *overidealized* male selfobject; if the MALE figure is *shorter* than the FEMALE, the sense is of *ambivalence* about gender identity with tendencies to *both defer* to the male selfobject and to *strive* to assert oneself.

When the FEMALE figure is drawn first.   If drawn by a *female* and the FEMALE figure is *taller* than the MALE, the sense is of the drawer's *uncertainty* about her gender identity, with feelings of *superiority* with regard to the male selfobject as part of the *compensatory structure* for this anxiety, if the FEMALE figure is *considerably shorter* than the MALE, again we have a sense of the drawer's *ambivalence* with conflicting tendencies to both *defer* to and strive to *assert* oneself vis-a-vis the male selfobject.

If drawn by a *male* and the FEMALE figure is *taller* than the MALE, the feeling conveyed is of the drawer's *anxiety* about his gender identity with a sense of *felt inferiority, inadequacy, and a passive-submissive* orientation toward the *overidealized* female selfobject; if the FEMALE figure is *shorter* than the MALE, the feeling conveyed is of *ambivalence* about one's gender identity with tendencies to *both defer* to the female selfobject and to *assert* oneself in relation to her.

Sexual Appearance of MALE and FEMALE Figures

Despite recent trends in unisex or androgynous styling in clothes, hair length, and jewelry, the usual tendency is for each gender to draw figures that are identifiable as males and females.

Although there may be some intermingling of traditional gender specific features, e.g., MALE figures being drawn with long hair and FEMALE figures wearing pants, if the *overall* impression in terms of facial features, clothing, body contours, and stance are those of a *feminine-appearing male* or a *masculine-appearing female*, the sense is of *ambivalence, ambiguity, and uncertainty* about gender identity, with the possibility of an *identification with the opposite gender* or the perception of identity problems in the selfobject of the opposite gender.

Optimal Expressiveness with Regard to the Whole Person

The different subjective connotations associated with the various presentations of the structure and type of the whole figure may be considered to be *optimally* represented if *all* of the following conditions have been met for *both* the achromatic and chromatic drawings.

With regard to *body configuration*, the subjective connection is to one's sense of *self-cohesion*. Optimally, the figure will have the *major areas*, (i.e., head, torso, limbs), *in proportion to each other*.

With regard to *body authenticity*, which relates to one's sense of *self-realization*, optimally, the figure will, in general, *conform* to average, acceptable physical dimensions for a person of the approximate age of the drawer or that of an identified selfobject.

In relation to *body image*, which refers to one's sense of *self-identity*, the figures will be similar to the drawer, identified selfobjects, or average adults in terms of age and size. They will be *moderately dressed*, (i.e., the figure must have appropriate covering of the torso and limbs indicated by a neckline, sleeveline, and cuff or hemline, and be wearing shoes), *not holding or surrounded by other objects*, and in an *upright, relaxed stance*, (i.e., front-face or slightly angled), or *moving or engaged in an activity in an easy, controlled manner*.

With regard to the *relationship of the MALE and FEMALE drawings*, which subjectively relate to the sense of *gender identity*, optimally, the drawer will draw *his or her gender first*. Both genders should draw the MALE and FEMALE of *equal height or the MALE slightly taller*. The *appearance* of the figures should generally *conform to contemporary societal standards* for males and females.

☐ E. OTHER FEATURES

Inquiry

The drawer is asked to respond to five questions with regard to both the MALE and FEMALE drawings (achromatic and chromatic):

1) Did you have somebody in mind? (or) Does he (she) remind you of anybody?
2) How old is this person?
3) What is he (she) doing?
4) What is he (she) thinking?
5) How is he (she) feeling?

Self versus Selfobject Reference

The answer to the first question will help to establish whether the interpretations pertain mainly to the drawer or a particular selfobject. Generally, whether or not the person of the opposite gender is specifically identified, the reference will be to a selfobject of that gender. If the drawer identifies the figure of the same gender as him or herself, it seems obvious that the reference is to the self. If, however, the figure of the same gender as the drawer is given a specific identity other than the drawer, the empathically derived interpretations will relate primarily to a selfobject of that gender, while references to the self may be derived both from that drawing and from the HOUSE and TREE drawings.

Age

The age of the PERSON(s) relate to the drawer's subjective sense of his (or the selfobject's) relative *maturity*.

Similar to the TREE, if the age given for a figure associated with the drawer or with a nonspecific selfobject is *within five years*, plus or minus, of the drawer's *real* age, an *optimal* sense of felt maturity may be inferred. If a specific selfobject has been identified, the same can be attributed with respect to that figure if the age given is *within five years*, plus or minus of that figure's *true* age.

If the age given is *more than five years less* than the drawer's (or the selfobject's) *real* age, the feeling conveyed is of a *lessened* sense of felt maturity. As the age given *decreases*, or the response given is "young" or "very young," that feeling has greater weight with an increasingly *regressive* sense of self.

If the age given is *more than five years over* the drawer's (or selfobject's) *real* age, the sense is of an attempt to *compensate for anxiety* with regard to her felt-maturity. As the age given *increases* over the drawer's real age, or the response given is "old" or "very old," the feeling evoked is one of *diminished* capacity with accompanying *depressiveness.*

Behavior

Normally, the response given to the question regarding the figure's behavior will coincide with the appearance of the drawn figure. *Optimally,* any activity that is described as *assertive or expressive* but is *nonviolent* in nature, e.g., walking, talking, smiling, playing ball, chopping wood, conveys a *vital* sense of self.

If the figure is described in a *neutral* way, i.e., not engaged in any activity or expressiveness, e.g., "doing nothing," "just standing (or lying or sitting) there," "just thinking," the sense is of *felt passivity, inhibition, and constriction.*

When the activity is described in *deprecatory* terms, e.g., "he's lazy," the sense is of *diminished self-esteem.*

Descriptions of *violent* activity convey feelings of *aggressiveness* with the possibility of feelings of *hostility* and *difficulties with impulse control.*

If the figure is described as *nonhuman,* e.g., a drawing or a statue, the sense is of a *diminished* sense of self-identity.

If the behavior is described as the performance of any activity that is *bizarre or weird,* the sense is of a continuum ranging from *immaturity and oppositionalism* to a *disturbed sense of reality* with the possibility of a *thinking disorder,* depending on the severity of the response.

Thinking

An *optimal* response will involve an expression of what the figure is thinking that is *pleasant or constructive* in nature, e.g., about a job, activities, or friends. The subjective connotation is of a *healthy* sense of self.

Responses that are *negative or deprecatory* of self or others give a feeling of *diminished self-esteem* with *felt depressiveness and/or hostility.*

When the figure is described as *"not thinking anything,"* the sense is of *evasiveness* with underlying *passivity and withdrawal.*

Bizarre or weird thoughts, similar to that described for behavior, elicit a sense of anything from *immaturity and oppositionalism* to a *thinking disorder* depending on the severity of the response.

Feeling

The *affective state* attributed to the figures elicits similar reactions to those described for cognitive activity.

Optimally, the figures will be described as having feelings that are *pleasant and constructive* in nature, connoting a *benign* sense of self.

Dysphoric feelings, e.g., sad or unhappy, convey *depressiveness and low self-esteem* as do *self-deprecatory* feelings, e.g., "he feels foolish."

Aggressive feelings, e.g., "she's angry," elicit a sense of *hostile-aggressiveness*.

When the figure is described as *"not feeling anything,"* the sense is of *evasiveness* with underlying *passivity, withdrawal, and depressiveness.*

Bizarre or weird feelings again suggest anything from *immaturity and oppositionalism* to *impaired reality orientation* depending on the severity of the response.

At times, a *mixed* response will be given, i.e., feelings will be described as *both positive and negative*. The sense is of *uncertainty* in a *poorly defined* self with a propensity for *mood swings*.

On the occasions that the impressions of the examiner with regard to the age, behavior, thinking, and feeling of the figures are markedly at variance with the responses given by the drawer, the most compelling meaning of this discrepancy may be the similarity to other instances of interpersonal communication in the drawer's life in which there is difficulty in establishing an empathic intersubjective connection.

☐ An Example of a Structural Analysis of the Persons

The Case of T. Y.

T. Y., a tall, attractive 35-year-old woman presented herself for psychotherapy as an eating-disordered (recovering bulimic), depressed person. A married mother of two young girls, she felt overwhelmed by daily responsibilities. In and out of therapy for the previous 10 years, she was aware that her perfectionism, addictive tendencies, saying "yes" when she meant "no," stemmed from a family in which her father was a cold, controlling perfectionist given to drinking and rages while her mother was passive-submissive. T. Y. still suffered from guilt with regard to her teenage sexual promiscuity.

Looking at T. Y.'s achromatic FEMALE and MALE drawings (Figures 6.59 and 6.60), done about one month after she began weekly therapy sessions, we are immediately struck by the fact that the figures are nude. Before reacting to this as it relates to the whole figure, let us proceed with a structural analysis of the separate features.

First, with regard to the pencil FEMALE's head, it seems to be small in relation to the size of the body. This suggests feelings of inadequacy with regard to intellectual ability with resultant passive, inhibited, or with-

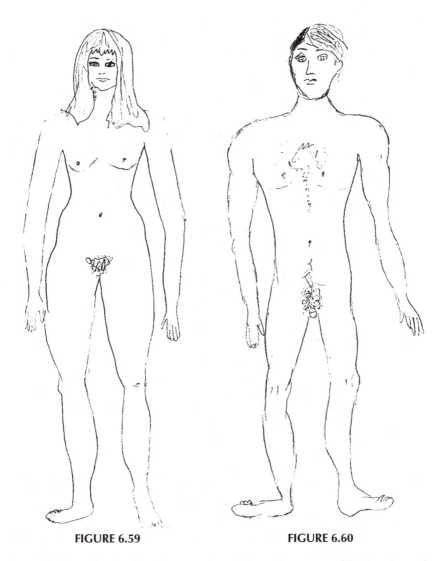

FIGURE 6.59   **FIGURE 6.60**

drawn behavior. The faint line quality adds to the sense of hesitancy and uncertainty.

In contrast, the eyes are relatively heavily drawn and large with accentuated pupils conveying feelings of tension and hypersensitivity with respect to receiving or conveying affective stimuli. The careful elaboration of the lashes points to perfectionistic and exhibitionistic structures that T. Y. has developed to compensate for her felt inadequacy. "If I look sexy and attractive perhaps I won't be rejected for my stupidity."

The lightly-drawn, small nose adds a sense of avoidance and passivity.

Completing the picture, the faint, smallish mouth tells us that T. Y. defends herself with regard to affective interaction with sources of selfobject gratification by avoiding or withdrawing from contact with consequent feelings of helplessness and hopelessness.

Similar to the way T. Y. drew the eyes, the more defined hair, drawn with moderate line pressure suggests that she overcompensates for her anxiety about how sexually desirable she is by exhibitionistic fantasies. Why fantasy as opposed to overt behavior? The overall faint line quality of the figure suggests an introversive rather than an extroversive orientation.

Moving to the torso, the pencil female's neck, indicative of her ability to integrate her thoughts, fantasies, and actions reveals some darker shading, suggesting anxiety in this area.

The very faintly drawn shoulders indicate great doubt and uncertainty in the area of taking on responsibility.

In contrast, the trunk, i.e., the area between the collar bone and the crotch, is more definitely drawn and moderate in size and shape, suggesting an underlying feeling of strength about her body.

Again, in contrast, the breasts are both faintly drawn and small for the size of the figure. This ties in with the faintly drawn shoulders in terms of T. Y.'s feelings of inadequacy in the role of mother, i.e., as a source of dependency gratification. Her experience of her mother as an inadequate source of both mirroring and idealization may also be reflected in how she drew the FEMALE's breasts. Also, struggling with her sense of sexual attractiveness, drawing the breasts exposed, but in such a faint manner, indicates her ambivalence about exhibitionistic compensatory strivings and uncertainty about her gender identity.

T. Y.'s drawing of the pubic area, overtly but with scribbled lines, furthers the sense of avoidant anxiety with regard to her sexual capability and her insecurity about her gender identity. Again, the compensatory structure involves exhibitionistic tendencies.

The overly large hips strengthen the finding that the drawing reveals an overcompensation for the anxiety she experiences with regard to her identity as a female.

With regard to the pencil FEMALE figure's limbs, one is struck by the faint, almost invisible, way T. Y. drew the arms and hands. This suggests tremendous doubt, indecision, and uncertainty about connecting with and controlling the environment. However, the overly long length of the arms points to a tendency to overcompensate for felt inadequacy by being overactive, i.e., extending herself too far.

In contrast, the legs are for the most part moderate in line quality, size, and shape indicating a sense of being able to maneuver in the world.

The figure's feet, however, are quite faint, pointing to her uncertainty

COLOR PLATE 1

COLOR PLATE 2

COLOR PLATE 4

COLOR PLATE 3

COLOR PLATE 6

COLOR PLATE 5

COLOR PLATE 8

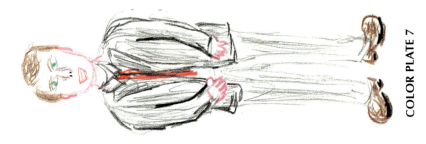

COLOR PLATE 7

COLOR PLATE 10

COLOR PLATE 9

COLOR PLATE 11

COLOR PLATE 12

COLOR PLATE 13

COLOR PLATE 14

COLOR PLATE 15

COLOR PLATE 16

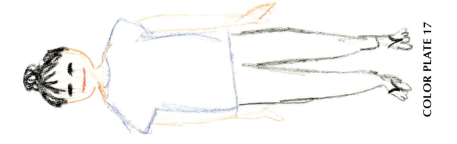

COLOR PLATE 17

COLOR PLATE 18

BIRD

COLOR PLATE 19

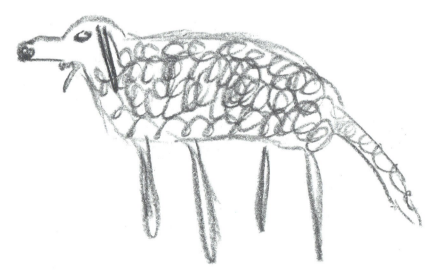

COLOR PLATE 20

COLOR PLATE 22

COLOR PLATE 21

COLOR PLATE 23

COLOR PLATE 24

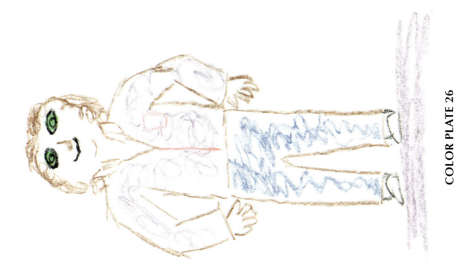

COLOR PLATE 26

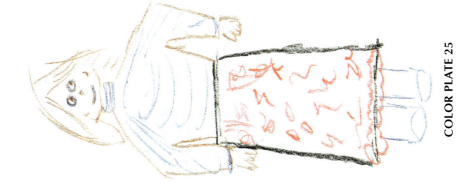

COLOR PLATE 25

COLOR PLATE 27

COLOR PLATE 28

COLOR PLATE 29

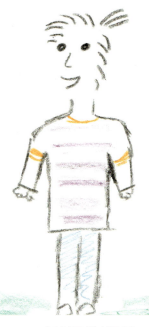

COLOR PLATE 30

COLOR PLATE 31

COLOR PLATE 32

about achieving a position of relative autonomy. This is underlined by the cutting off of one foot that adds a sense of constriction and inhibition.

The very large size of the whole figure conveys a sense of an excessive effort to be noticed as a way of compensating for feelings of inadequacy.

The imbalance of the major areas of the body, i.e., small head, long arms, large hips, points to a lack of felt self-cohesion. On the other hand, there is a very real-looking quality to the drawing suggesting a strong sense that what she is expressing about herself is how she truly experiences it as opposed to a fantasy projection.

Again, presenting the figure as totally nude evokes the sense of exhibitionistic overcompensation for feelings of inadequacy and insecurity with reference to being a woman. The stance of the figure, on the other hand, seems to say, assertively, "This is me. I'm not hiding anything."

With regard to the inquiry, the age of the figure, 36, and self-referential responses make it clear that the figure represents herself. The response, "Just standing with my body," conveys feelings of passivity and inhibition. Nevertheless, the desire to be seen (known) is reflected in her response to the question of the figure's nudity: "I'm exposing myself." The feeling of being "very uncomfortable" adds a dysphoric tone and her basic ambivalence is reflected by the response, "Part of me is O.K. and part is unacceptable."

Contrasting T. Y.'s chromatic FEMALE drawing (Color Plate 15) with the achromatic figure, we get the impression that they were drawn by two different people. Whereas the latter has a veridical, almost photographic quality, the former appears haphazard and distorted. This points to a split between T. Y.'s conscious, here-and-now self-image and an affect-driven conception, less concerned with "reality" and defensive and compensatory structures and more reflective of deeper fears and insecurities.

These two drawings illustrate a *vertical split* (Kohut, 1971, 1977), in which the self is divided both horizontally and vertically. The chromatic drawing represents a vertically split off self-organization, the result of early and continued narcissistic deprivation during which her parents failed to respond to her authentic, independent narcissistic strivings. The drawing represents the compensatory and defensive structures that the patient developed in an effort to maintain attachment to these significant selfobjects. In T. Y.'s case, her father responded to her living out his grandiose-exhibitionistic needs, not her own. Her mother offered little active resistance to the father's domination and was an inadequate source of mirroring and idealization in her own right.

The achromatic drawing represents T. Y.'s attempt to disavow (i.e., "split" from) this inauthentically experienced self-organization. The sexual exhibitionism and overstriving of the achromatic figure represent an effort to achieve recognition in the here-and-now "real" world as her "true" self. However, the depletion of energy caused by the split on her attempt to be her own self can be seen in the faint line quality of the achromatic drawing.

Chapter VIII will provide further explanation and illustration of the "vertical split."

With regard to T. Y.'s crayon FEMALE's head, the sense of intellectual inadequacy, presented in a passive, hesitant manner in the pencil drawing, is replaced by tremendous tension and avoidant anxiety. The profile presentation elicits feelings of evasiveness and avoidance. The large, heavily reinforced eye adds a sense of hypersensitive suspicion and guardedness. T. Y., presented with the selfobject milieu of color, i.e., affective stimulation, reveals her fear of affective interaction, as evidenced by the tiny nose and chin and reinforced, slash-like, unsmiling mouth. The carefully modulated pencil presentation of the hair in color is presented as a disarrayed mass indicative of her sense of poor control and low self-esteem with regard to her sexuality. The use of red for the face, reinforced and drawn over, conveys both the wish and fear associated with being an active person who draws notice to herself.

The chromatic female's neck, faint in outline but invaded by a heavy slash from the chest, suggests the intrusion of bodily impulses causing anxiety about her ability to control inner urges.

Similar to the achromatic FEMALE, T. Y. again conveys a sense of bodily strength indicated by a sturdily drawn torso. However, the torso can be seen to resemble a bottle (leading up to the funnel-like neck). The repetitive, heavy horizontal stripes can be seen as bars. The overall effect is one of containment, of "bottling up" this inner energy lest it break loose. The two heavy lines drawn in the breast area resulting in no breasts suggest her powerful underlying need to deny her role as a source of dependency gratification and her sexual attractiveness.

The extremely heavy shading of the crotch area reinforces the sense of anxiety about her sexual adequacy. The extra reinforcement of the buttocks relates this anxiety to uncertainty about her gender identity. Looking at the torso alone, there is not much to suggest a female figure. These findings underlie the suggestion of sexual trauma at an early age, i.e., being forced to relate to a powerful selfobject for the gratification of his needs, which lead to the formation of a vertically split self-organization.

Turning to the limbs, the arms are overly long and distorted, the right being too thin and the left, too thick. This conveys feelings of ambivalence with regard to the ability to connect with others. On the one hand T. Y. feels inadequate and passive. On the other, there is a sense of blunt aggressiveness. The excessive length suggests overcompensation in the form of excessive activity. In any case, the distorted right hand and missing left hand convey a gross sense of inability to control her interactions. Therapy revealed that this reflected her actual frustration with regard to her difficulty in dealing with her children, i.e., feelings of helpless ineffectuality on the one hand versus severe guilt due to inability to control her rage reactions (mainly verbal) on the other.

With regard to the figure's legs, the right one is fairly evenly drawn but the left is too long, mostly thin and distorted. This represents a startling contrast from the achromatic figure's sturdy, well-shaped legs. So the everyday sense of being able to maneuver in the world is contrasted, on the affective level, with a discrepancy, similar to the arms, which points to ambivalence, with both passive (right side = more "normal") and aggressive (left side = more "regressive") tendencies. The line quality and shape of the right and left feet are consistent with this splitting as it relates to relative autonomy.

The size of the crayon figure, though smaller than the pencil FEMALE, is still quite large pointing to overcompensation for felt inadequacy. This figure's head is more in balance with the body but the overly long limbs belie the sense of self-cohesion.

The relative distortion of the features, on the affective level, indicates that T. Y.'s sense of control is less intact when exposed to this kind of stimulation.

Her sense of who she is moves from someone who will appear to reveal everything in order to be noticed to one who presents only one side of herself but attempts to shore up her sense of identity by feeling like an active, assertive person seeking her own receptive environment. The heavily drawn green of the tree leaves gives a sense of the tension underlying this effort.

The inquiry bears out the desire for a setting in which to be active as a way of restoring her sense of self. She states that the figure is "Thirty. Running—jogging on the beach. Just enjoying being by the ocean, the open space. Feels good."

T. Y.'s achromatic drawing of the MALE figure (Figure 6.60) is very similar in size and line quality to the FEMALE. Turning first to the inquiry, the responses seem to indicate that the figure is meant to represent her husband whom she wants to join her in "exposing" himself but whom she perceives as reticent and uncomfortable in the process of self-revelation. The figure is described as "Thirty-five. More unwillingly standing there. He says, 'I want to have my clothes back on.' He doesn't feel comfortable at all." This corresponds to T. Y.'s description of her husband as an unemotional, withholding person.

As a potential source of selfobject gratification, T. Y. makes some important distinctions between herself and this figure. First, the pencil MALE's head is larger than the FEMALE's and more in proportion to the rest of the body. Thus, she seems to experience him as being more intellectually capable. However, the reinforced outline of the head points to T. Y. perceiving him as anxious about his ability. The very faint features add to her sense of him being hesitant and withdrawn in terms of his capacity to receive and react to emotional stimuli.

The MALE's hair is more heavily shaded on the right side, sketchier on the left, but with an overly neat, contained appearance. The feeling is of tension and ambivalence with regard to the MALE's sexual desirability and sexual capacity.

The figure's overly wide neck suggests a sense of preoccupation with issues of mind-body control. Again, this seems to coincide with T. Y.'s description of her husband as inflexible and domineering.

The MALE's shoulders are sturdy looking but faintly drawn, suggesting that her perception of her husband is that he has the capacity to shoulder responsibility but is uncertain about his ability. There seems to be even less confidence with regard to his ability to connect with and control his environment as evidenced by the thin and faintly drawn arms. Again, the outline of the torso is moderately drawn indicating a basic sense of adequacy about the figure but the faint, thin legs and feet point to a perception of the MALE figure as inadequate to maneuver and take a relatively autonomous stance in the world.

The tiny penis adds to the feeling that T. Y. experiences her man as sexually inadequate and overly inhibited.

The whole figure is so lightly drawn that the overriding sense is that T. Y. experiences her husband as making even less impact than she does. The disproportionately large shoulders suggest that she perceives him as devoting an excessively large amount of his energies to taking on responsibility. This coincides with her description of him being more involved with his career than the concerns of the family.

This here-and-now presentation of the man in her life is in stark contrast with the chromatic depiction (Color Plate 16), similar to the discrepancy between the two FEMALE drawings. Here, however, the color MALE figure appears to be better balanced and contained than the chromatic FEMALE. The inquiry provides the information that he is "Forty. Sitting on a porch swing. Enjoying reading and relaxing. Feels content, relaxed." The heavy shading of the whole figure evokes a sense of strain, pressure, and tension but the size and shape of the head, trunk, and limbs elicits the impression that, in terms of more fundamental affective capacity, T. Y. experiences the male as being more cohesive and stronger than the female. The transparency of the hands and book, the very heavy shading of the right hand and the claw-like left hand draw attention to an area of distortion with regard to her perception of the male's ability to exert control. T. Y. may have drawn the figure in a passive, seated pose and consigned the hands to a passive activity because on the deeper, affective level that the chromatic experience affords, she is afraid of the male's potential for violence. The way the torso is "boxed in" also points to her attempt to contain his inner strength. Even though seated, the overall size of the chromatic MALE is equal to that of the FEMALE.

In summary, the MALE and FEMALE drawings obtained shortly after T. Y. entered therapy reveal a woman who has a tremendous sense of inadequacy. On a more conscious, day-to-day level, she manifests compensatory and defensive structures that focus on activity and sexual attractiveness but that still leave her feeling hesitant and uncertain. On this level, she presents the selfobject as more intellectually capable and responsible but equally vague and hesitant and even less willing to expose himself.

The color drawings, which tap a deeper emotional dimension, although presenting "clothed" figures, strip away much of the compensatory veneer. With regard to herself, the color FEMALE reveals tremendous anxiety about her basic inner strength, sexuality, aggression, and capacity to "face the world" and connect with and perform in it. With regard to the MALE, she appears to perceive this figure as more capable than the FEMALE but she has strong, underlying fear of his aggressivity and a need to neutralize his potential for harmful loss of control. Much of this relates to the father of her childhood who was capable of causing her terrible empathic wounding.

Turning now to the drawings done by T. Y. after approximately 14 months of mostly twice weekly dynamically oriented psychotherapy, which took as a cue from the initial set of drawings the patient's need for a strong idealized selfobject transference with the therapist whose empathic acceptance could serve as a buttress against her inner sense of inadequacy and fear of loss of control, the structural analysis points to some rather significant changes.

To begin with, and most obviously, the achromatic FEMALE figure (Figure 6.61), is now clothed. Apparently, T. Y. no longer has the need to "expose" herself in the hope of being noticed. What may be of greater significance is the line quality of most of the figure.

Compared to the initial FEMALE, (Figure 6.61), the line pressure has a moderate, firm feel. The only departure from this involves the shoulders and the left forearm.

Taking it from the top, the head and facial features appear more defined indicating that T. Y.'s sense of being able to receive and react to emotional stimuli has improved considerably. The figure's eyes, though still prominent, do not have the reinforced pupils of the first drawing which are associated with hypersensitivity and suspiciousness. Furthermore, the size of the head is larger and more proportioned to the rest of the body indicating a greater sense of intellectual adequacy. The shading and shaping of the hair appears more natural than the first drawing suggesting an easier approach to feelings concerning attractiveness or sexual desirability, but the heavier shading on the left side of the head suggests a degree of continued anxiety in this area.

The heavily drawn vertical line for the neck on the same side also points to concerns about control.

The faintly drawn shoulders indicate that T. Y. remains uncertain about her ability to handle responsibility but less so than the practically invisible shoulders of the first drawing indicated.

Moving down the figure, the wide expanse of the dress as it covers the hips and upper legs implies concern about this area of the body. Looking very carefully, we see that T. Y. erased and widened the right side of the dress indicating self-criticality. The effect is to take away from the slimness of the figure rendering it less sexually attractive.

The sense of effectance, of being able to connect with the world, seems to be manifested by the size and shape of the arms, particularly the right one. Inner conflict about acting out inappropriately may account, though, for the erasure (break in continuity) of the left forearm.

With regard to the ability to control the environment, associated with the drawing of the hands, we find the partial concealment of the right hand by the left. This can be seen as the representation of ambivalence about reaching out and actively pursuing a goal. The pose of the figure is quite demure and the hands can also be seen as forming a "pelvic defense," i.e., a barrier against sexual intrusion. This combination of erasures, concealments, and postures all suggest that in the here-and-now world represented by the achromatic phase, T. Y. is still struggling, albeit with a more definite sense of self, with her sexuality. If she no longer has the urge to overcompensate for felt inadequacy by exhibitionistic means, how then to relate to the world as a sexually mature person? The responses to the inquiry bear out T. Y.'s state of confusion. She states that the figure is "looking blandly into space—thinking and feeling confused." The younger age of the second achromatic figure, 25, also suggests the wish to be less connected to her true age and the responsibilities that go with it but also to have more of a chance to restructure herself.

Finally, the firm sketchy line quality and graceful pose of the lower legs indicate a greater sense of being able to maneuver toward her goals while the feet, one heavily reinforced and resting on the base of the page, the other cut off, suggest that she remains insecure, ambivalent, and needful of support with regard to adopting a position of relative autonomy.

Similar to the contrast between the achromatic and chromatic first set of FEMALE figures, the two of the second set are markedly different. However, where the pencil drawing is still overly large and precise, the

FIGURE 6.61   **FIGURE 6.62**

second crayon FEMALE (Color Plate 17) is more moderate in size. The medium of affective expression (color) now seems to be approached in a less pressured, more casual manner. These findings reflect an increased level of self-acceptance. This "vertically split" self appears to represent a great improvement over the one evidenced at the beginning of therapy when given the opportunity for affective expression.

Structurally, the head is of more than adequate size. The choice of orange, with moderate line quality and subtle shading, are clear improvements over the first crayon FEMALE. However, the heavily drawn slitted eyes and the absence of ears and a nose, indicate that T. Y. remains fearful of affective interaction with others. The large, somewhat smiling mouth is a definite improvement over the first chromatic FEMALE. The hair, pulled up in a bun, appears to indicate a desire to contain her preoccupation with sexual attractiveness, but the heavy line quality betrays the continuation of anxiety in this area.

T. Y.'s very short, somewhat disconnected neck for the second crayon FEMALE is markedly different from the first. The desire to distance herself from bodily impulses seems to have been replaced by a greater willingness to confront control issues but with continued anxiety, which is now replaced by a passive, reflective stance instead of an overly active one. This impression is reinforced when we view the arms, (the right drawn in a weak, limp, faint way; the left, somewhat stronger looking but still faint and immobile), and consider the inquiry response as to what the figure is doing and feeling: "(She is) 40, thinking about her house, (and feeling) overwhelmed."

Of interest is T. Y.'s treatment of the second crayon FEMALE's shoulders: the right one appears quite adequate while the left appears to be drooping with the burdens of responsibility.

This figure's upper body could be that of a male. She seems to still feel inadequate as a woman in terms of functioning as a mother. Underlying wishes to have the freedom of a young male may also be manifested in this manner. The extended line joining the legs at the crotch may also reflect a conflict over her gender identity.

A nascent awareness and focusing of the ability to control the world may be seen in the sharply drawn left hand, the line pressure and shape suggesting an underlying aggresivity. Note the contrast with the weak, faint right hand: the "correct" (right) side = feelings of inadequacy; the "sinister" (left) side = "don't mess with me!"

Vast improvement seems to be in evidence with regard to the sturdy looking legs and feet. Under conditions encouraging affective expression, T. Y. seems to be readier to maneuver and stand on her own feet. However, the heavily drawn "V's" of the sandals suggest a degree of tension about achieving greater autonomy.

The two MALE drawings also appear to be greatly contrasted. Echoing the achromatic FEMALE, the pencil MALE (Figure 6.62), is clothed and drawn with mostly moderate or firm sketchy line quality.

If the selfobject reference is still T. Y.'s husband, there is a vast improvement in the perception of him as a pleasant, attractive figure. The relative smallness of the head in relation to the size of the body may indicate a deemphasis of his intellectual capacity. In keeping with this, the somewhat moderately shaded and attractively styled hair and the addition of a mustache conforms to her report that she experiences him as more sexually desirable. The other features: the bright, moderately line pressured eyes, the adequate nose, and the smiling mouth convey a sense of friendliness and approachability. This is in general keeping with T. Y.'s communication in therapy of an improved relationship with her husband. The heavily drawn ear and reinforced chin (left side of face) and faintly drawn chin (right side of face) point to her perception of him as somewhat hypersensitive and ambivalent about his assertiveness.

The same pattern of line quality for the neck as for the chin suggests a mixed view of his capacity for control. However, the size of the neck is clearly more moderate in the second achromatic MALE drawing as are the shoulders.

The rest of the torso and limbs are quite large and in proportion to each other but not to the head. It is as if T. Y. experiences her husband as being quite capable in terms of strength, ability to connect, to maneuver, and to stand on his own feet but to be out-of-sync, to lack the cohesion to be able to integrate his dreams and wishes with this capability. The inquiry reveals him to be younger than the first drawing, 25, "thinking about his future but feeling 'bottled up,' " i.e., lacking the clear planning and sense of effectance to actualize himself. This finding is furthered by the partially concealed hands in pockets which convey a sense of ambivalence, constriction, and inhibition with regard to the ability to control the environment. The faintly drawn midline strip of buttons also indicates T. Y.'s uncertainty about his degree of dependency. The very faint right forearm adds to the sense of uncertainty about his ability to make meaningful connections. All of these findings reflect T. Y.'s reports bearing on her husband's indecisiveness about his career coinciding with success in his job.

The great contrast of the second chromatic MALE (Color Plate 18), with both the second pencil MALE and the first chromatic, reveals the extent of the split between T. Y.'s here-and-now self and selfobject configurations and what emerges when given the opportunity for affective expression. The moderate size and relaxed stance of the second crayon MALE, the sensitively modulated shading of the torso and legs, the happy facial expression and positive, hopeful tone of the inquiry, ("A teenager, 15. Enjoying life. Waving—socializing. Thinking about what he's going to be doing, what he wants to do. Feels great."), all point to the wish for the kind of freedom and opportunity for fulfilling life experience that she never experienced as a teenager. T. Y. attributes these qualities to the male role. This figure may represent an unconscious merger with the male selfobject. The existence of anxiety accompanying these feelings appears in the heavy shading and "wild" quality of the hair, the slitted eyes which do not permit the figure to really see what is out there, the heavy brown line for the right side of the neck, and especially, the use of yellow for the outline of the head and the arms and hands. Yellow, used appropriately, conveys a sense of aspiration, relaxation, and spontaneity. In this drawing, however, the effect is to render those outlines hardly visible suggesting T. Y.'s great ambivalence about her intellectual ability and her capacity to reach out to connect with and control the environment.

In summary, the two sets of drawings may be seen to reflect both T. Y.'s progress after over one year in therapy and areas that remained problematic. From a person whose self-perception in the day-to-day, "black-and-white" world featured excessive preoccupation on her physical/sexual self as a way to compensate for a deep sense of inadequacy, she was able to ameliorate the uncertainty and inhibition that accompanied this self-image and to reflect a firmer, more positive picture. The "vertically split" self-configuration, given expression by the opportunity to use color to reveal wishes, fears, and feelings that could not be expressed in the mundane black and white sphere of expression, transformed from a tense, distorted, escapist figure to a more controlled, capable, and relatively autonomous figure though still burdened and inhibited.

Her perception of the main source of selfobject gratification, her husband, underwent a similar transformation. From her initial presentation of him in the here-and-now world as an overly responsible though inhibited figure, unresponsive to her needs, she later presented him as a highly attractive figure who remained somewhat stifled and uncertain about his capability and direction. The "split" figure, given the opportunity for affective expression, appeared to reveal the release of merger wishes with the male role expressing her capacity for joyous, youthful expression, but still accompanied by uncertainty about her ability to connect with and function in the world. These drawings both reflected and confirmed trends observed in the course of therapy and indicated areas of self-development that remained to be explored.

Structural Analysis–The Animal

The ANIMAL drawing may be considered to be a projection of more archaic, primal, or primitive, underlying, developmentally early aspects of the person's inner self or, correspondingly, the more primitive aspects of a relevant source of selfobject involvement.

The relevant features of the ANIMAL include:

A. The Head
B. The Torso
C. The Limbs
D. The Tail
E. The Whole Animal
F. Other Features

☐ A. The HEAD

An animal's head, in contrast to a human's, does not connote, subjectively, a reference to cognitive activity. Rather than complex inner process such as intellectual functioning or fantasy, one is drawn to surface characteristics to determine potentials for aggression, approachability, friendliness, etc. Furthermore, an animal uses its sense organs (eyes, ears, and nose) with greater intensity and its mouth for more functional purposes than a human. These qualities may then be considered to be aspects of *relatedness to or interacting with the environment* which encompasses *receiving and reacting to affective stimuli* on a relatively more *primitive, early, or raw* experiential level.

Omission

When the head is *concealed,* e.g., behind an object, the feeling evoked is of *anxiety* about relating with a tendency to *avoid or evade* primitive involvement with the world.

Not drawing the head conveys a more *severe* reaction to a deep fear of relating on a primal level. The feeling elicited is of *extreme withdrawal* with the possibility of a *thinking disorder.*

Size and Shape

An *overly large* head, (i.e., head is disproportionately long and/or wide relative to the size of the body for the type of ANIMAL drawn), conveys a sense of *overcompensation for anxiety* with regard to archaic relating. The reaction is of *overinvolvement* with the environment.

An *overly small* head, (i.e., head is disproportionately short and/or narrow relative to the size of the body for the type of ANIMAL drawn), elicits the feeling of *inadequacy* with regard to primal interreacting with the world with consequent *passive, inhibited, or withdrawn* behavior.

A head that has *irregular contours* or a shape that is *distinctly inappropriate* for the type of ANIMAL drawn evokes feelings of a *distorted* reaction to relating in a primitive fashion and raises the possibility of a *thinking or neurological disorder.*

Connection of Head to Body

When the *head is not connected to the body*, the feeling is of *severe breakdown* in the individual's capacity to relate to the environment and his bodily impulses in a primitive manner. This evokes the possibility of *dissociated behavior and/or a thinking or neurological* disorder.

Position

It is not uncommon for the head of the ANIMAL to be drawn in profile or angled as well as frontally viewed. When the head is presented *rearview,* the sense is of a rather *severe withdrawal* from primal interpersonal relatedness.

Mouth or Beak

The ANIMAL's *mouth* may be indicated by one or two connected or unconnected curved or straight lines, by a shaded area, or by some type of circle or oval drawn within the head. The *beak* may be indicated by a projecting structure from the head, usually cone-shaped or pointed.

The animal uses its mouth to communicate, to gain nourishment, to defend itself or attack, and to manipulate and carry objects. These functions represent a primary means of relating to the world. The drawn ANIMAL's mouth then elicits feelings related to basic archaic ways of *interacting* with the environment.

Omission

If the mouth or beak is *concealed,* the subjective sense is of *anxiety* about primitive relations with a defensive reaction of *evasion.*

Not drawing the mouth or beak elicits the more extreme feeling of *withdrawing* from interaction.

Size

An *overly large* mouth or beak, (i.e., disproportionately wide and/or long relative to the size of the head for the type of ANIMAL drawn), elicits a feeling of *overcompensating for anxiety* about relating in a raw, basic manner with a tendency to be *overactive.*

An *overly small* mouth or beak, (i.e., disproportionately narrow and/or short relative to the size of the head for the type of ANIMAL drawn), evokes *felt inadequacy* in the context of relating to the world in an archaic manner with defensive reactions of *passivity, inhibition, or withdrawal.*

Expression

When the mouth is *open and turned down at the corners,* the impression is of *"menace"* and conveys a sense of *hostile-aggression* as a way of expressing primitive relatedness (see Figure 7.1).

Teeth or Fangs

These may be indicated by lines within or extending outside of the mouth area. *Prominent and/or sharp or jagged* teeth or fangs convey a

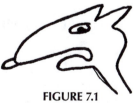

FIGURE 7.1

sense of *hostile-aggressiveness* with respect to primal interaction with the environment.

Eyes

Eyes can be drawn as an outline and pupil or filled-in circle or oval or in a manner appropriate to the type of ANIMAL drawn. Similar to the human figure, the drawing of eyes relates, subjectively, to how one *receives and reacts to affective stimuli*. In the case of the ANIMAL, though, this dimension of interreacting to the environment conveys a sense of *raw, primal* experience.

Omission

It is not unusual for only one eye to be drawn in an angled or profiled figure.

When *one eye is concealed* in a front-view figure, the sense is of *anxiety* defended against by *avoidance or evasion* with regard to the threatening stimuli. If *both eyes are concealed*, the *severity* of the reaction is emphasized.

If *one eye is simply not drawn* in a front-view presentation, the sense is of *ambivalence* about receiving or reacting to emotional stimuli on a primitive level with a tendency to be *both withdrawn and aware*.

If *one eye in an angled or profiled* figure or *both eyes in a front view* are *not drawn*, the feeling evoked is of even greater *withdrawal* with the possibility of a *thinking or neurological disorder.*

Size

Overly large eyes, (i.e., disproportionately large relative to the size of the head for the type of ANIMAL drawn), convey a feeling of primitive *hypersensitivity.*

Overly small eyes, (i.e., disproportionately small relative to the size of the head for the type of ANIMAL drawn), elicit feelings of primitive *avoidance and withdrawal.*

Shape and Composition

Eyes that are drawn as an *outline only with pupils omitted* convey a sense of *anxiety* about primal interreaction with the environment defended against by *withdrawing* into the self.

Where eyes are drawn as *dots or circles totally filled in, as slits or as closed,* the feeling elicited is also of *anxiety* with the defensive reaction pointing to primitive *avoidance or denial* as well as *withdrawal*.

A *narrow and slanted* shape of the ANIMAL's eyes evokes a *"menacing"* feeling giving a sense of *raw hostility* with regard to interreacting with the environment in a primitive way (see Figure 7.2).

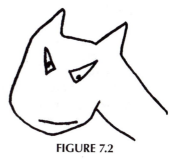

FIGURE 7.2

Ears

Ears include the outer and inner area in a manner appropriate to the *type* of ANIMAL drawn. They should be considered only for ANIMALS normally depicted with ears.

Similar to the ANIMAL's eyes, the drawn ears refer, subjectively, to how the individual *interreacts with the world on a relatively primitive level with respect to affective stimuli*.

Omission

Again, it is common for *only one ear* to be drawn in an *angled or profiled figure*.

When *one ear is concealed in a front-view* figure, feelings of basic *anxiety* about receiving and reacting to affective stimuli are elicited and defended against by primitive *avoidance or evasion*. *Both ears concealed intensify* this reaction.

If *one ear is not drawn in a front-view* figure, the sense is of *ambivalence* with *awareness* countered by *withdrawal* tendencies.

If *one ear in an angled or profiled* figure or *both ears in a front view* are not drawn, the sense is of *severe withdrawal*.

Size

Similar to the eyes, *overly large* ears elicit feelings of raw *hypersensitivity*, while *overly small* ears convey feelings of primitive *avoidance and withdrawal* with regard to receiving or reacting to affective stimuli.

Shape

Ears that come to a *sharp point* convey a feeling of raw *hostility* with regard to interreacting vis-a-vis affective stimuli.

Nose or Snout

This feature may be drawn as lines or a shaded area, either within the face or projected out from the head, in a manner appropriate to the *type* of ANIMAL drawn.

The sense of smell is particularly important to the animal. The drawing of the ANIMAL's nose conveys, subjectively, a *developmentally early sense of the way one receives and reacts to affective stimuli*.

Omission

If the nose is *concealed*, the sense is of an *anxiety* about basic interreacting with affective stimuli, defended against by a primitive *avoidant or evasive* reaction.

Not drawing the ANIMAL's nose evokes a more severe defensive reaction encompassing *withdrawal*.

Size

An *overly large* nose or snout, (i.e., disproportionately wide and/or long relative to the size of the head for the type of ANIMAL drawn), evokes a sense of primitive *hypersensitivity* with regard to receiving and reacting to affective stimuli.

An *overly small* nose or snout, (i.e., disproportionately narrow and/or short relative to the size of the head for the type of ANIMAL drawn), elicits feelings of primitive *avoidance and withdrawal*.

Optimal Expressiveness with Regard to the Head and its Features

For the ANIMAL's entire head and its eyes, ears, nose (or snout), and mouth (or beak) to be depicted in a way that conveys a sense of *optimal* relatedness and capacity to receive and react to affective stimuli in a primitive manner, *all* of the following conditions should be met for *both* the achromatic and chromatic drawings:

> the *head, mouth, nose, eye(s), and ear(s)* should have *moderate* line quality and shading;
> *color appropriate* to the *type of ANIMAL* should be used;
> the entire head, the eye(s), the ear(s), the mouth (or beak), and the nose (or snout) should be of *moderate* size and shape (proportionate to the size and shape of the *whole* body or head, respectively, for the type of ANIMAL drawn);

the *head should be attached to the torso* and *not drawn rear view*;
the *mouth should be straight or upturned*;
the *teeth or fangs should be omitted or not drawn in a prominent and/or sharp or jagged manner.*

☐ B. The TORSO

Subjectively, one reacts to the animal's torso, i.e., the body exclusive of the head and limbs, as the source of *primitive strength or force.*

Omission

Concealing the torso evokes a sense of *anxiety* about the expression of primitive strength defended against by *avoidance and evasion.*
    Not drawing the torso *intensifies* this reaction.

Size

An *overly large* torso, (i.e., disproportionately long and/or wide relative to the other body parts for the type of ANIMAL drawn), elicits a feeling of *overcompensating for anxiety* about manifesting primitive strength by being *exhibitionistic or domineering.*
    An *overly small* torso, (i.e., disproportionately short and/or narrow relative to the other body parts for the type of ANIMAL drawn), evokes a sense of defending against the *fear* of expressing archaic force by being *passive, inhibited, and/or withdrawn.*
    A torso with *irregular contours* or a shape that is *distinctly inappropriate for the type* of ANIMAL drawn evokes a sense of *distortion* with regard to the manifestation of one's primitive strength. This raises the possibility of a *thinking or neurological disorder.*

Optimally, the way in which the drawing of the ANIMAL's torso would reflect the individual's feelings about her primitive strength would involve (for *both* the achromatic and chromatic drawings):

moderate line quality and shading;
color appropriate to the *type* of ANIMAL drawn;
moderate size (proportionate to the size and shape of the whole body for the *type* of ANIMAL drawn.

☐ C. The LIMBS

The limbs may be shown as: 1) *legs,* which would be seen as extensions from the torso including, at their end, *feet, hooves, paws, or claws;* 2) *wings or fins* that would include the *entire area* leaving the torso.

Similar to the arms and legs of the human, the limbs of the ANIMAL evoke, subjectively, a sense of the individual's capacity to approach and escape from sources of gratification and danger, respectively. Also, the connotations of attack and defense ("flight or fight") are associated with the ANIMAL's limbs. With the ANIMAL, though, there is an added dimension of range and power, e.g., "thundering hooves," "soaring wings." These associations combine to elicit a sense of raw, basic capacity to connect with, control, and maneuver in the world, i.e., being involved with the environment in a primitive manner. Which of these subjective implications is ascendant in a particular drawing will depend, in part, on the *type* of ANIMAL drawn.

Omission of Limbs

Some ANIMALS are normally depicted without limbs, e.g., a snake. For ANIMALS that are normally drawn with limbs, when *one or more of the limbs is (are) fully concealed*, the sense is of *ambivalence* with regard to issues of primitive connection with, control of, and/or maneuvering in the world.

If *one or more of the limbs is (are) incompletely drawn, partially concealed, or partially cut off by an edge of the page*, feelings of *constriction and inhibition* are elicited.

If *all of the limbs are fully concealed*, the sense is of more *severe resistance* and *evasiveness* to being primitively involved with the world.

If they are *all incompletely drawn, partially concealed, or partially cut off by an edge of the page*, the feelings of *constriction and inhibition are intensified*.

When *one or more of the limbs is (are) not drawn*, again, the sense is of *ambivalence* about primitive involvement with the world, but with a more *severe* response indicating that the thought process is *partially blocked*.

When *all of the limbs are not drawn*, the feelings conveyed involve a primitive sense of *helplessness and inadequacy* with resulting *depression and withdrawal*.

Size and Shape of Limbs

Overly large limbs, (i.e., disproportionately long and/or wide relative to the size of the body for the *type* of ANIMAL drawn), convey a sense of *overcompensation for felt inadequacy* with regard to basic functioning in the world by a reaction of *overactivity or over striving*.

Overly small limbs, (i.e., disproportionately short and/or narrow relative to the size of the body for the *type* of ANIMAL drawn), convey the drawer's sense of basic *inadequacy, inhibition, and passivity* with regard to connecting with, controlling, or maneuvering in the environment.

Limbs that are drawn as *single lines* convey a sense of *severe felt inadequacy*.

Unequal size or asymmetrical limbs, (i.e., some limbs are disproportionate in size or shape relative to the other limbs), elicit feelings of *ambivalence* with regard to primitive functioning involving *both passive and assertive or aggressive* tendencies. *Extreme dis-*

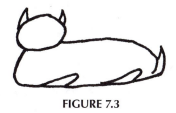

FIGURE 7.3

crepancies suggest the possibility of a *neurological disorder or mental retardation*.

When the *feet, hooves, paws, or claws* are drawn in a *"menacing"* way, i.e., they are *unusually sharp, pointy, or spiked* for the *type* of ANIMAL drawn or are drawn in a *threatening* manner or position, the feeling conveyed is one of raw, *hostile-aggressiveness*.

Position

Limbs that are *contained within or positioned tightly against* the ANIMAL's body convey a sense of *rigidity and constriction* with regard to primitive functioning in the environment (see Figure 7.3).

Limbs that are *fully detached from the torso* elicit a feeling of *severe anxiety* with regard to primitive functioning in the world. This kind of *perceptual distortion* conveys the sense that the individual is capable of *dissociated* behavioral reactions.

When limbs are drawn *touching the base of the page*, the sense is of *strong felt insecurity and constriction* with regard to primitive functioning in the world.

☐ D. The TAIL

The tail of an animal is generally depicted as an appendage extending from the rear of the torso, whose function serves as a mood indicator, e.g., a dog's wagging tail indicating friendliness, and as a feature that enhances or detracts from the animal's aesthetic appeal. Subjectively, for the drawer, the ANIMAL's tail conveys a sense of *primal affective mood or tone*. The common expressions, "having your tail between your legs," which indicates a dejected or humiliated state, or "walking with one's tail up," which indicates a state of good spirits or cheerfulness, are illustrative of this vicarious connotation. A further subjective connection may be indicated by the colloquial reference for the female as "a piece of tail." The positioning of the tail near the buttocks and anus lends further support for the meaning of the ANIMAL's tail to have reference to one's own or a selfobject's *primitive sexual capability or desirability*.

Omission

When the tail is *not drawn or is concealed* for ANIMALS normally depicted with one, the sense is of *anxiety* with regard to revealing one's primal affective mood and/or making reference to one's sexual prowess. The distinction, if any, will depend on the type, size, and position of the ANIMAL. This anxiety is defended against by *avoidance and evasion*.

Size

An *overly large* tail, (i.e., disproportionately long and/or wide relative to the size of the body for the *type* of ANIMAL drawn), conveys a feeling of *overcompensation for anxiety* with regard to revealing one's underlying mood or sexual capacity with tendencies toward *overactivity or exhibitionism*.

An *overly small* tail, (i.e., disproportionately short and/or narrow relative to the size of the body for the *type* of ANIMAL drawn), conveys the drawer's *felt inadequacy, passivity, and inhibition* with respect to revealing primal moods or feelings about sexual capability.

Position

A tail that is *contained within or positioned tightly against* the ANIMAL's body elicits feelings of basic *rigidity and constriction*.

If the tail is *fully detached from the torso*, the sense is of *anxiety* with regard to revealing primitive affects or expressing archaic sexual feelings with the possibility of *dissociative* affective or sexual reactions.

Optimal Expressiveness with Regard to the Limbs and Tail

To convey a sense of *optimal* capacity to connect with, control, or maneuver in the environment on a primal level as revealed by the ANIMAL's limbs and to indicate primitive affective mood and/or sexual capability or desirability as revealed by the tail, *all* of the following conditions should be met for *both* the achromatic and chromatic drawings:

> *moderate* line quality and shading;
> *color appropriate* to the *type* of ANIMAL;
> *moderate* size and shape (proportionate to the size and shape of the torso and head for the *type* of ANIMAL drawn);

limbs and tail should be *attached to the torso* at the *appropriate places* and *not contained within or held tightly against* the ANIMAL's body.

□ E. The WHOLE ANIMAL

Similar to the human figures, the *whole* ANIMAL provides insight into aspects of self-experience but in the latter case, on an underlying, primitive, developmentally early level.

Body Configuration

With regard to the ANIMAL, the manner in which the head, torso, limbs, and tail are balanced relates, subjectively, to the sense of *self-cohesion* with reference to *primal affective and behavioral* aspects of the individual's experience.

Optimally, the ANIMAL will have the head, torso, limbs, and tail in proportion to each other. Subjectively, this elicits a feeling of *self-cohesion* with respect to primitive affective and behavioral potentials.

When the figure is *out-of-balance*, (i.e., the head, torso, limbs, and tail are *not* in proper proportion to each other with regard to the *type* of ANIMAL drawn), the sense is of a *lack of self-cohesion* with regard to primal affects and behaviors with compensatory and defensive structures focused on the features that are distorted (see Figure 7.4).

If the figure is drawn in a *grossly disproportionate* manner, (i.e., it is *extremely out of conformance* to the basic proportions of the ANIMAL named with regard to the size and shape of its parts), the sense is of a *severe disturbance in reality perception* with reference to the way that the primitive affects and behaviors should cohere in the person. This raises the possibility of a *thinking or neurological disorder* (see Figure 7.5).

If the ANIMAL is drawn in an *asymmetrical* manner, (i.e., one side is *extremely disproportionate* in size and shape from the other side), one senses a *split* in the drawer's experience of inner cohesion with possibility of a *dissociated* reaction.

DOG

FIGURE 7.4

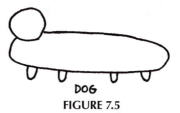

DOG

FIGURE 7.5

Body Authenticity

The way the person draws the *whole* ANIMAL in terms of its conformity to what is generally accepted as its usual physical dimensions, (i.e., how *authentic* it looks), reflects, subjectively, on the sense of how *real* one feels oneself to be when dealing with underlying primitive affects and behavioral potentials.

Optimally, the drawn ANIMAL will look like the animal that the drawer names. This points to a sense of inner reality when experiencing primitive affects and behavioral urges.

When a *stick figure* is drawn, the sense is of experiencing oneself as *unsubstantial and inadequate* in dealing with primal affects and behavior. The defensive reaction involves *oppositionalism and evasion.*

A *blank outline,* (i.e., a whole figure is outlined with no inner features), elicits a sense of *severe evasion, withdrawal, and depressiveness* in the face of a *diminished* sense of self-realization when dealing with primitive feelings.

A *primitive* figure, (i.e., simple, barely differentiated shapes for the body parts with minimal details), evokes a *highly regressed, undeveloped* sense of self and suggests a *thinking or neurological disorder or mental retardation* in the context of experiencing primal, underlying affects and behaviors.

If the ANIMAL is drawn as a *geometric* figure, (i.e., squares, circles, etc. are used for the parts), again we have a sense of *impaired reality perception* in terms of the person's feelings of being "real" in the context of dealing with primitive affects and behavior. This also evokes the possibility of a *thinking or neurological disorder or mental retardation.*

A *bizarre or grotesque* ANIMAL, (i.e., the figure is drawn in a weird or monstrous way), elicits a feeling of *severe, underlying disturbance* with elements of *fear and rage* in the individual's reality sense and again suggests a *thinking or neurological disorder.*

When the ANIMAL is *fantastic or whimsical* (without being bizarre or grotesque), the feeling conveyed is of an *altered* sense of self-reality when dealing with primitive affects and behavioral urges. If the resultant drawing evokes an *appealing* reaction, the sense is of a capacity for *originality.* If it is *not appealing,* the feeling is one of *nonconformity or oppositionalism.*

An *anthropomorphized* ANIMAL, (i.e., the ANIMAL has *human-like* features), elicits feelings of a *severe blocking* of primal experience with powerful *evasive and avoidant* measures necessary to maintain a sense of reality.

Position

The stance or movement of the ANIMAL provides a sense of the drawer's potential for *interacting with the environment* in the context of experiencing one's primitive affective and behavioral tendencies.

Usually, the ANIMAL is drawn in a *upright, motionless* position.

When depicted in some form of *nonaggressive movement,* (e.g., walking, running, climbing, flying, etc.), the sense is of an *optimally active, assertive, interactive* potential.

An *aggressive, nonviolent* movement or stance, (e.g., leaping, rearing up, etc.), elicits a feeling of *aggressiveness.*

Violent movement or stance, (e.g., attacking, biting, having bared fangs, coiled as if to strike, etc.), conveys a *hostile* feeling with the suggestion of a *potential for loss of control* of primitive rage impulses.

When the ANIMAL is drawn as *slanting or leaning,* the sense is of feelings of *uncertainty and insecurity* about interacting.

A *floating* figure elicits a feeling of *detachment and avoidance* with regard to interacting in the context of experiencing one's primitive urges.

A *reclining* ANIMAL evokes a sense of *passivity* in that context.

☐ F. OTHER FEATURES

Inquiry

The drawer is asked to name the *type* of ANIMAL drawn and to give its *age.*

Type

There are common, colloquial associations to different kinds of animals. The kind or type of ANIMAL selected by the drawer may relate, then, to the overall subjective characterization she has with regard to her (or that of a significant selfobject's) underlying primal, affective, and behavioral potential. This will be modified by the *way* the ANIMAL is drawn.

Drawing a *dog or a cat* evokes the feeling that the drawer wants to *normalize* his primitive potentials in order to present a picture of *conformity.*

A *horse* elicits feelings of *strength and helpfulness.*

Birds in flight, subjectively, may relate to a wish to *transcend* one's ordinary experience, to *escape.* A *seated or perched bird* may reflect the feeling of being *frustrated* in that wish, of being *tied down.*

Owls are associated with *wisdom* and *parrots* with the ability to talk, i.e., to *verbalize* primitive impulses.

Worms, mice, and insects, (if not harmful), convey a sense of *weakness,* of *felt inadequacy.*

Elephants, rabbits, panda bears, sheep (or lambs), cows, birds, or fowl not associated with flight (e.g., chickens), herbivores (e.g., giraffes), fantastic or whimsical animals (if not in violent action) evoke a sense of *nonassertiveness.*

Fish are associated with *passivity.*

Carnivores (e.g., *lions, tigers [if not in violent action], dolphins*), elicit the feeling of *assertiveness.*

Carnivores, if in violent action, are associated with *aggressiveness.*

Snakes, rats, spiders (or other harmful insects), sharks, bats, fantastic ANI-MALS *(if in violent action)* convey a sense of *hostile aggression.*

Age

The age ascribed to the ANIMAL relates, subjectively, to how *mature* the drawer experiences himself (or a significant selfobject) to be, with regard to control over primitive affects and behavior.

Commonly, an animal's age is equated with a human's on a ratio of *one year* of the former's age being equivalent to *seven years* of the latter's.

Optimally, then, if the age given for the ANIMAL is between *three and nine* years or the ANIMAL is labeled as *"adult" or "mature,"* the sense is of a feeling of mature control over primal experience.

If the age is given as *under three years* or the ANIMAL is stated to be *"young" or a "baby,"* the feeling elicited is of a *lessened* sense of felt maturity with potential *regressiveness* with regard to control over primitive affects and behavior.

If the age is given as *more than nine years* or the ANIMAL is called *"old" or "very old,"* the feeling evoked is one of *diminished* capacity in terms of the expression of primitive affects and behavior with a sense of *constriction* and *depressiveness* superceding that of felt maturity.

☐ An Example of a Structural Analysis of the Animal

The Case of K. X.

K. X., a 20-year-old college dropout, entered therapy at his parent's insistence. They were "fed up" with his "laziness" and secretive behavior. Currently working in his father's factory, the latter described his son as acting like "a dummy, a patsy" while on the job. The father, a tough, self-made, successful businessman, was impatient with and rejecting of his son. Their relationship was acrimonious. The mother, though equally frustrated by her son's lack of achievement, tended to be softer and more protective of him, shielding him from his father's angry tirades. She stated that he had never "produced" in school and was the class clown.

K. X., a middle child with a married older sister and a younger brother who was successful in school, felt that he was constantly being compared

FIGURE 7.6

unfavorably to his siblings. He revealed that he never liked to take orders and liked to do anything but read and do schoolwork. At his father's business he felt that the other workers were "out to get" him because he was the boss' son.

K. X. entered weekly therapy and quickly revealed that he had a rather serious drug problem, mainly marijuana and qualudes.

Figure 7.6 and Color Plate 19 show K. X.'s achromatic and chromatic ANIMAL drawings, respectively, done shortly after he began therapy. A structural analysis of the pencil drawing, a snake, provides an insight into the patient's primitive affects and behavioral tendencies as he presents himself to and experiences the world on a here-and-now, surface level.

The most striking features of the head area are the eye and mouth. The narrow, elongated shape and heavy, dark line quality evoke a chilling sense of menace and the feeling of raw hostility with which K. X. views the world. The indication that the figure refers more to himself than to a selfobject is reinforced by the age given in the inquiry for the snake as being "young, one or two years."

The mouth appears to be overly elongated even for the type of ANI-MAL drawn, suggesting that with regard to basic, primal ways of inter-acting with the environment, K. X. overcompensates for anxiety by being overactive. The absence of fangs lessens the sense of overtly aggressive behavior, however.

These findings correspond to the patient's reports of rage towards his father, envy toward his siblings, and an avid preoccupation with satisfy-ing his craving for drugs.

The elongated torso adds a sense of compensatory exhibitionism to the picture of a person with strong underlying anxiety (heavily drawn lines and reinforced shading) about unleashing primitive power. The position of the body, recoiling back on itself, gives a feeling of the snake being ready to defend itself if attacked, rather than coiled and ready to strike. In the absence of limbs, this seems to describe K. X.'s way of interacting with the world: alert to danger, adopting a menacing pose but concen-trating his energy and power on defense as opposed to maneuvering freely in the world.

The heavily drawn, sharply pointed "rattle" at the end of the tail again draws our attention to K. X.'s tension and aggressive tone with regard to his need to defend himself from danger, possibly by scaring those whom he perceives as potentially harmful. The tail also provides a sense of the interweaving of aggression into K. X.'s sexual experience.

With regard to the patient's sense of how real he feels himself to be when experiencing these primitive affective and behavioral tendencies, the whole snake gives a veridical feeling. However, K. X. states that he "started out to draw a giraffe, then a bird." This elicits a sense of the passivity and vulnerability that underlie the hostile-aggressive pose that K. X. adopts when he confronts what is for him a dangerous, ungiving world. The young age of the snake reinforces the sense of felt immaturity and a regressive wish for the anxiety-free state that drugs provide him.

K. X.'s chromatic ANIMAL, a bird, permits an exploration of primal affective and behavioral tendencies in the context of stimuli that touch a deeper, more affectively complex level of experience.

Does this drawing relate primarily to the self or a significant selfobject? This evaluator is struck by the size and pose of the figure which convey a sense of imperiousness. This, in addition to the age given as three years as opposed to the snake being only one, induces the sense that K. X. is ac-tively projecting feelings about his father in the color drawing as well as revealing his own self-state via identification with the selfobject. In the absence of optimal mirroring from his father, K. X. appears to have compensated by idealizing his father with respect to those traits which give the appearance of strength.

We again find that the eyes and mouth figure prominently in eliciting a sense of the hostile and actively aggressive manner in which K. X. experiences both his father and himself to interact with the world and each other. Unlike the snake, though, the bird's eye has no pupil. This underlines the sense that K. X., on a deeper emotional level, defends himself against the anxiety and depression he experiences in interacting with the world by withdrawing from it. This, in addition to the extreme tension indicated by the heavy black line for the mouth point to K. X.'s anxiety about ingesting drugs in order to achieve some form of release.

The use of yellow at the beak, the only color besides black to be employed, adds to the sense of a desire for release from unendurable burdens and restrictions.

Next, we are drawn to the extended length of the torso. This ties in with the feeling of imperiousness which led to an identification of this figure with the father selfobject. It can be said that K. X., in experiencing anxiety about how both he and his father manifest raw power, overcompensates by making this feature more prominent, conveying tendencies toward both exhibitionism and domination.

With respect to the limbs, the extended size of the wings also lends to the sense of overcompensation for felt inadequacy with regard to basic functioning in the world. The transparency evident in the body line being able to be seen through the wing suggests that rather than a severe breakdown of reality testing, K. X. added the wing after he drew the body. It seems that in his desire to extend its length, he disregarded the reality constraint of what was already established. This could be analogous to how K. X., in his deep need to find gratification, disregards rules and makes errors in judgment.

The heavily drawn "feet" of the bird, which are also too small to sustain such a large body, attest to the underlying tension and feelings of inadequacy, inhibition, and passivity he experiences with regard to connecting with, controlling, or maneuvering in the world.

This is a bird that is not ready to fly but to make a menacing presence. There is a lack of felt cohesion in terms of a sense of inner balance among his feelings, urges, and abilities. However, as suggested by the size of the figure, the age of three being consonant in human terms with his own age (20), and the feeling of real expressiveness in the "look" of the figure, the sense is that this drawing reflects a true picture on a deep emotional level of how K. X. feels about himself and a significant selfobject. The tone of dysphoria, dissatisfaction, and depression conveyed by the predominant use of black, characterized K. X.'s basic state of being as he entered psychotherapy.

FIGURE 7.7

What do we find after one year of weekly psychotherapy that was aimed at providing a predominantly empathic, noncritical experience?

K. X.'s achromatic drawing (see Figure 7.7) is now a fish. The feeling of hostile aggressiveness conveyed by the snake is totally absent. The eye is large with a reinforced pupil eliciting a sense of hypervigilance. Combined with the position and expression of the lips, the feeling is of eagerness to make contact with sources of primal gratification. The large size of the body with its moderate, casual shading provides a sense of K. X.'s being comfortable with exerting his energies in that direction. The heavy shading of the upper fin-like projections and the sharp points of the lower, interject a reminder of the anxiety and aggressive potential that K. X. brought to his interface with the environment at the beginning of therapy. The heavily drawn line quality of the tail also elicits a feeling of tension, possibly with regard to his feelings about sexual capability or desirability. Nevertheless, the overall subjective quality of this six-month-old fish as a cute, passively unthreatening creature prevails.

As reported in therapy, K. X. did experience a lessening of angry interaction with his father. However, he still used drugs, primarily to quell his anxiety and enable him to function socially and in his sexual relationship with his girlfriend.

The chromatic drawing of a dog (Color Plate 20) carries out the sense of a transition from the hostile, domineering impact of the chromatic bird at the beginning of therapy to a more benign expression of primal need. Nevertheless, on this deeper level of affective expression, considerable anxiety and tension characterize K. X.'s experience.

The elongated and heavily drawn snout and the reinforced nose elicit a sense of severe tension and hypersensitivity with regard to reacting to primitive affective involvement. The heavily drawn vacant eye and overly elongated, darkened ear reinforce this sense of hypersensitivity and protective reaction of withdrawing. The mouth, on the other hand, conveys a sense of readiness for involvement. K. X. craves gratification but remains guarded and suspicious as he seeks it out.

The torso, quite large in relation to the head, is filled with scribbled lines that convey an underlying quality of felt inadequacy or uncertainty about basic strength.

The legs are heavily reinforced and overly long suggesting great anxiety but also an urge to overcome this anxiety to maneuver in the world. Considering that this is the first attempt to depict the capacity to function in the environment, the effort to draw limbs may be seen as the expression of a deep desire to be less passive in achieving gratification of basic needs. Still, the detachment of one limb from the body, which indicates the potential for dissociation, and the lack of outlined paws, which give a sense of blunt, undifferentiated action, reinforce the sense of K. X.'s potential for raw, maladaptive behavior.

The elongated tail drawn in a drooping position, combined with the overall heavy line quality of the black color and the age given as seven, much older (in human terms) than K. X.'s real age, all suggest a sense of lessened capacity and depression.

While he strives to normalize his approach to experiencing his deeper affective and behavioral needs, K. X. feels himself to be suffused with anxiety and tension in approaching the real world.

What we appear to see reflected in the ANIMAL drawings is a young man who entered therapy with a character armor of hostile aggression with overcompensatory mechanisms to deflect the anxiety related to his powerful sense of inadequacy who, after a year in which he felt sufficiently buoyed by an empathic selfobject, could relate to his primitive potential as experienced in the day-to-day environment in a relatively passive, open manner. On a deeper affective level, he could express the tremendous anxiety he experiences as he attempts to find gratification for these needs as a normal functioning person.

The "Vertical Split" as Seen in Projective Drawings

In the discussion of the human figure drawings of T. Y., the concept of the *"vertical split"* was introduced.

Kohut first elaborated on this concept in *The Analysis of the Self* (1971). He explained that the narcissistic energies, (exhibitionism and grandiosity), which flow upward in the child toward expression may be "co-opted," in effect, by the parental selfobject who makes the price of connection the substitution of his own narcissistic needs as opposed to the recognition of the child's independent strivings. In such cases, the child forms a separate self-organization derived from the selfobject's strivings which exists side-by-side with his own. The effort to disavow this "other" self leaves the self-organization connected to the reality ego, which does not receive mirroring or the opportunity for idealization or twinship, depleted and subject to the experience of low self-esteem, isolation, lack of initiative, and depression. Kohut states that we are dealing with the side-by-side existence of cohesive personality attitudes with different goal structures, different pleasure aims, and different moral and aesthetic values.

Bacal and Newman (1990) relate Kohut's *"vertical split"* to Winnicott's *"false self"* and the *"illusory me-you relationship"* of Sullivan and to aspects of Fairburn's and Guntrip's schizoid personality formations.

Bacal and Newman state that these splits represent failures in the original developmental experiences of the child and reflect a desperate need to relate to the selfobject at whatever cost in order to maintain a self-organization and to defend against unmanageable affects.

Goldberg (1995), in his explication of perverse sexual behavior, incorporates Kohut's *"vertical split,"* i.e., one part of the psyche harbors perverse activity while living apart yet side-by-side with the reality ego. Like Bacal and Newman, he states that a split is demanded in order to stay connected to the parent, a sustaining selfobject. One part of the self participates in a grandiose, exhibitionistic display with an archaic or infantile selfobject, while another is oblivious to this behavior. The *"vertical split"* allows the perverse sector to operate as if it were a separate personality. Sexual excitement is the "remedy" for a depleted self, i.e., one that has not received empathic attunement from a responsive selfobject. Goldberg points out that the split ranges from the normal to the overtly psychotic.

By identifying a "vertical split" early in treatment via projective drawings, the therapist is enabled to recognize seemingly incongruent, inconsistent behavior and to focus his efforts in healing the split by empathically attuning to the *patient's* underlying grandiose-exhibitionistic needs.

Indications of the presence of a "vertical split" are found when the achromatic drawing is characterized by evidence of a depleted self-structure and the chromatic drawing reveals structural elements that stand in marked contrast to it in terms of affective energy.

Retesting after a period of time in therapy permits the therapist to assess the extent to which integration has taken place. The need to provide the patient with the opportunity to reveal a vertical split by the use of both achromatic and chromatic drawings for the HOUSE, TREE, PERSONS, and ANIMAL is underscored.

☐ An Example of the *"Vertical Split"*

The Case of I. D.

I. D.'s TREE drawings were previously presented as an example of a structural analysis of the TREE (Chapter 5). It will be remembered that I. D., a 46-year-old recently unemployed, divorced man, presented with anxiety and depression related to his failed marriage and job loss.

I. D.'s initial TREE drawings revealed great differences between the achromatic (Figure 5.32) and chromatic (Color Plate 13) drawings. The impression then was that the two drawings looked as if they had been drawn by different people. The pencil TREE reflected anxiety in dealing with the environment, a felt lack of strength, and minimal sense of stability, security, or insight. In contrast, the TREE drawn with crayons looked vital, strong, and mature, with an optimal sense of stability and connectedness.

The lack of congruence between these two drawings suggests the presence of a vertical split in which the chromatic drawing represents the manifestation of grandiose-exhibitionistic energy, which formed into a coherent self-organization in the context of a selfobject milieu that provided an outlet for a full range of affective expression. The fact that this is a compensatory structure is seen when we empathically relate to the achromatic TREE drawing and experience a sense of disorganization, disconnection, and weakness. Deprived of selfobject support, this self-organization reveals the depletion of energy with which I. D. confronts the here-and-now "real" world.

After one year of therapy, the achromatic TREE (Figure 5.33) revealed that I. D. manifested a more differentiated, though still far from optimal capacity to interact with the environment. His sense of inner strength still reflected anxiety and uncertainty but seemed to be more connected with his ability to relate. The presence of a groundline gave some sense of the patient's feeling that he had a foundation of inner support when confronting the "real" world. The chromatic TREE (Color Plate 14), though still stronger looking than the achromatic, did not appear as vibrant as the first chromatic TREE. It no longer presented as optimal a picture of grandiose-exhibitionistic energy.

What may be reflected by the changes in the drawings is the result of therapeutic attunement to I. D.'s on-going, day-to-day selfobject needs.

Thus, after a year of psychotherapy, we appear to see less depletion in the self-organization that relates to here-and-now "reality" experience and a corresponding weakening of the grandiose-exhibitionistic energy invested in the self-organization that becomes manifested when given the opportunity for a greater range of affective expression.

Turning to I. D.'s drawings of a MALE figure, done at the beginning

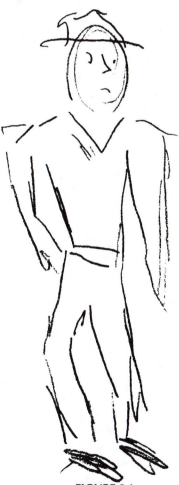

FIGURE 8.1

of therapy, we find a startling difference, parallel to that of the TREE, between the achromatic and chromatic figures (Figure 8.1 and Color Plate 21, respectively). The former impresses as a weak, passive, disjointed figure while the latter appears vibrant, strong, and decisive. Structurally, the head of the pencil MALE conveys a sense of avoidant anxiety with regard to I. D.'s feelings of intellectual adequacy. Drawing a hat suggests an attempt to defend against anxiety about his capability by concealment, but this in turn causes tension and a loosening of reality testing (transparency). The tiny eyes and absence of ears point to withdrawal from affective interaction while the small, downturned mouth give a distinct feeling of dysphoria and withdrawal. The absence of a chin reinforces the sense of severe nonassertiveness while the absence of a neck reinforces the sense of I. D.'s wish to avoid dealing with the need to integrate mind and body because of gross felt inadequacy.

A fragmented sense of being able to take on responsibilities is accompanied by anxiety with regard to the patient's feeling of inadequate inner strength and sexual capacity and ability to control the latter.

Marked anxiety and ambivalence about connecting with the world is revealed by the heavily reinforced, unequal-sized arms. The concealment and omission of the hands conveys I. D.'s sense of profound felt inadequacy and constriction about exerting control.

The weak-sketchy line quality of the legs evokes the feelings of hesitancy and uncertainty with which I. D. attempts to get around in the world. The distortion of the right leg makes it look as if he is being pulled back to the past, which in effect cripples his ability to maneuver effectively. Finally, the sense of severe anxiety about achieving autonomy is reflected by the heavy shading of the feet. The detachment of the right foot from the distorted right leg along with the thinner right arm and concealed right hand evoke a sense of I. D.'s potential for unintegrated, possibly irrational behavior.

Turning to the chromatic MALE (Color Plate 21), we find a figure that appears to be as full of a sense of confidence as the achromatic one was replete with felt inadequacy. Structurally, this figure reveals far fewer of the less-than-optimal indicators of the figure that related to the monochromatic day-to-day "real" world. Side-by-side with this figure we find a "business man" dressed for power and success. However, I. D. states that the figure is a bit worried about the economy giving some indication that the chromatic MALE is not without uncertainty. The concealed hands and heavily reinforced face and shoes also betray tension about facing the world and standing on one's own in it. These findings point to the anxiety underlying the compensatory facade of the "vertically split" self-organization.

During the course of treatment, it was revealed that I. D.'s parents' marriage was marked by violent fights. His father drank heavily and virtually ignored him as a young child. His mother, a "loner" with few friends, led him to believe that his conception was a mistake. (His parents were relatively older when he was born.) The one thing that impressed his parents was his success in school and graduating from college, something his older siblings had never accomplished. I. D. learned to rely on his charm and wit to achieve mirroring from other adults. This is where his grandiose-exhibitionistic energy went, leaving little left for that part of him that had never experienced selfobject recognition.

FIGURE 8.2

When we examine I. D.'s drawings of the MALE figure after one year of therapy, we find a stronger, more integrated achromatic figure (Figure 8.2).

The hair is no longer concealed beneath a hat, the mouth is smiling, the head is connected to the body, (albeit with anxiety), at least one shoulder is squared, and, significantly, the arms are of equal size and the hands are revealed indicating a sense of being able, not without anxiety, to connect with and control the environment. The figure is described as "35, content, relaxing, and thinking about the girl he is going out with that night." The availability of narcissistic energy to the figure related to here-and-now reality suggests a breaching of the vertical split. The chromatic figure (Color Plate 22), now reveals, more openly and extensively, some of the anxiety I. D. experiences about receiving and reacting to affective stimulation and connecting with others. The similarity in body configuration and posture further the sense of integration of the patient's self-organization.

9

CHAPTER

A Complete Impressionistic and Structural Analysis

This final chapter will bring together what has been advanced in the previous sections, with regard to the application of a self psychological approach to the understanding of projective drawings.

☐ The Case of C. N.

C. N., a 30-year-old divorced dentist, entered therapy at the urging of his current girlfriend. Their relationship was marked by an "on-again, off-again" pattern, with C. N. the one who initiated both the breakups and reconciliations. In therapy, he began by elaborating on his relationship with an abusive older sister who was more popular than he and who never let him forget how inadequate he was. He felt unsupported by his parents who did not see the "emotional abuse" he endured from his sister.

C. N. described his father as an unemotional person who stayed away from controversy until forced to take a stand. He was totally unlike C. N.'s mother who felt inferior to her siblings and, subsequently, was highly opinionated, stuck her nose into everyone's business, and promoted herself by tearing down others. C. N. remembered little twinship experience with his father who was thin and athletic, while C. N. was heavy and clumsy as a child. In contrast, his mother took considerable interest in his academic achievement but took the credit for it.

153

In his marriage, C. N. came to experience his wife as a selfish person, much like his mother and sister. She was withholding of affection, unlike his present girlfriend. Any indication of distancing by the latter, however, was experienced as a severe empathic break, leading to his pulling away.

C. N. realized that his experience with the main female selfobjects in his life made it difficult to believe that any woman could be trusted to be a consistently giving and affirming figure. On the other hand, C. N. had not internalized a capacity for self-soothing and a sense of inner strength as a result of his failure to form an idealizing selfobject relationship with his father. The primary goal of therapy, then, became the establishment of an idealizing selfobject transference, which would enable C. N. to absorb and overcome the disintegrative effects of the empathic wounds he experienced in his relationship with his girlfriend.

C. N.'s projective drawings, completed about one month after he entered therapy, initially impress with the degree of care and involvement he appeared to invest in the achromatic HOUSE (Figure 9.1).

The impression given by the achromatic HOUSE with regard to how C. N. relates to the selfobject milieu on a primary, face-to-face level and to what the drawing reflects with regard to self-structure, is primarily a favorable one. The drawing gives the feeling of being accessible, approachable, attractive, comfortable, creative, decorative, detailed, dignified, expansive, formal, friendly, lived-in, organized, precise, related, strong,

FIGURE 9.1

warm, and wealthy. However, the impression given by the side wall with the large chimney practically overpowering the main wall is of C. N.'s perspective being out-of-balance with the result that he has to crowd in the features that relate to making contact (e.g., door and windows). The feeling is of this part buckling under the weight of the overcrowding.

The structural analysis also conveys a sense of accessibility, but the careful elaboration of details of the door and the sheltering portico suggest underlying anxiety, which is compensated for by a compulsive orientation and exhibitionistic tendencies. Also, some ambivalence about being approached is conveyed by the short, compressed walkway.

The solid baseline and grounding give a sense of felt stability. However, the transparency of the baseline behind the hedges suggest lapses of judgment. The number, line quality. size, location, and detailing of the windows convey a very positive degree of relatedness with the outside world.

The wall lines, reflecting self-control, betray anxiety and insecurity. The huge side wall evokes a feeling that C. N. needs to present the side of himself that heavily features his preoccupation with warmth (the chimney), as much as he does the side that is capable of and involved with more differentiated interaction.

Except for the bottom roofline cutting through the chimney and windows, the roof elicits a sense of a strong inner cognitive life. Similar to the baseline, though, the transparent roofline may reflect occasional lapses of judgment.

The size and prominence of the chimney reveal the centrality of C. N.'s need for warm familial involvement. The lack of straightness, the line cutting the middle, transparency at the top of the chimney by the roofline and of the smoke, and the limited amount of smoke for the size of the chimney, all point to the difficulty C. N. has with this issue.

The addition of a deck and umbrella and the foliage along with the window flower boxes, give a sense of life and vitality to the drawing. C. N.'s answer to the question regarding what feeling the HOUSE gives, (i.e., "A warm, comfortable house. They enjoy relaxing on the deck in the warmer weather and curling up by the fireplace when it's cold."), reinforces that impression. The answer to the question concerning who lives in the HOUSE, (i.e., "A family: father, mother, child, (maybe not a child), reveals underlying uncertainty and insecurity about his position within the family, however.

When we examine C. N.'s chromatic drawing of a HOUSE (Color Plate 23), we obtain a considerably different sense of self-selfobject relatedness. The pencil drawing suggests that C. N. experiences his connection to his primary source of selfobject gratification, his family, as requiring a more elaborate, differentiated effort when functioning on a here-and-now, "real" level of involvement. When given an opportunity for a more regressive, affective level, afforded by the availability of color, the impressionistic analysis of the HOUSE still features it being accessible, alive, friendly, and warm but this HOUSE seems colorful, cute, modest, ordinary, simple, unaffected, and unassuming as opposed to the adjectives which reflected the more substantial achromatic structure.

Selfobject relationships in the "real," immediate world require greater intellectual effort. The looser and simpler quality of the chromatic drawing reveals a wish for a self-experience and selfobject relatedness that is easier, more relaxed.

As therapy progressed, C. N.'s revelations that he was tired of the constraints and requirements of running a dental practice, and his wish to relocate to a less urban area and find less demanding work, supported these findings from the initial HOUSE drawings.

Structurally, the chromatic HOUSE reveals a simpler door, done in a color, BLUE, that connotes calmness, peace, and tranquility. However, the faint line quality, the imprecise connectedness of the joints, and the carelessly drawn steps suggest uncertainty, ambivalence, and inconsistency with regard to how accessible C. N. really is on an affective level. The poor connection of the walkway to the HOUSE also conveys an ambivalence about being approached, as does the fact that it terminates facing the side rather than the bottom of the page.

Although the chromatic HOUSE has a baseline represented by foliage and an ample indication of grounding, the HOUSE appears to be floating above the ground conveying the feeling that C. N. does not experience the ability to make a fully stable connection with the environment.

The presence of only two windows, again sloppily drawn and placed mainly above the top of the door, reinforces the feeling of detachment or guardedness, of not wanting to fully interact with others.

The heavy line quality, lack of straightness of the wall lines, and lack of connection with the roof add to the impression of anxiety about self-control. Drawing only a single wall conveys the sense that C. N., given the opportunity for affective expression, reveals only a superficial view of himself. Underlying the elaborate picture he gives in the "real" world is a sense of wanting to exert much less effort to be connected to others.

Shading the roof with red, albeit faintly, suggests the presence of a wish for excitement and action underlying the peaceful facade.

The heavier use of red for the chimney and the heavy black smoke give a sense of the tension and intensity that accompany his longing for familial involvement.

The colorful flowers, foliage, and tree lend a happy, alive feeling to the drawing. Yet, the almost superfluous presence of a "red-headed" tree (mother?) suggests underlying anxiety about how to balance self and selfobject connectedness.

Nevertheless, C. N.'s responses to the inquiry reveal less conflict and more vitality, activity, and nurturance when reacting to the opportunity for a more expanded, affective response. He answered: "This is a family house—mother, father, two children. This is a fun place to live, the family plays together. It's a very warm, sweet, smiling place. Fresh things are baked here."

Moving to the TREE drawings done at the outset of therapy, the impressionistic analysis of the achromatic TREE (Figure 9.2) yields this list of adjectives: alive, aggressive, angry, assertive, (somewhat) barren and (somewhat) blooming, busy, confusing, detailed, different, dominating, elaborate, expansive, imaginative, mature, powerful, (somewhat) stark, solid, strong, tough, and unconventional.

FIGURE 9.2

Most of these impressions are derived from the BL area. Structurally, its large size in relation to the trunk, conveys a sense of overcompensating for anxiety about interacting with the environment by becoming excessively active. (This conforms with C. N.'s reported unhappiness with how overworked he felt.)

When we reflect on how the branches are bare at their base, (which evokes a sense of having little to offer), but become busy, overly organized, almost chaotic in their separate configurations as they reach the surface, we can feel C. N.'s essential ambivalence, i.e., wanting to be left alone but feeling compelled to interact.

The sharp, spiky, heavily pressured quality of the outermost branches and their separate club-like groupings convey a sense of hostile-aggressiveness that accompanies this compulsion to interact.

The fact that the BL area comes close to the edge of the page, but does not extend over it, exemplifies the feeling that C. N. has an urge to reach beyond the limits of his environment but contains or constricts himself.

With regard to the trunk, the relatively small size proportionate to the BL area, elicits the feeling that C. N. experiences himself as having insufficient inner strength to sustain all that frenzied, intricate interaction with the environment. The heavily drawn outer lines indicate the tension he feels in maintaining his strength and the slight lean of the trunk suggests a feeling of being weighed down.

The position of the knothole near the top of the trunk points to a fairly recent trauma, possibly his divorce. The sketchy line quality evokes a sense of how sensitive and tender this wound is to him.

C. N.'s TREE is clearly grounded but the lack of roots gives a feeling of unbalance to the whole structure—a flight into activity to avoid dealing with one's inner pain and longings? C. N. answers that the TREE is "100 to 200 years old" but "very alive." One gets the sense of him feeling both "tired out" and yet striving for vitality. Amplifying this, he states, "Spring leaves are just coming into once barren leaves."

Like the HOUSE drawings, having to relate to the "real," black and white world evokes a sense of a great expenditure of effort by C. N. When we turn to the chromatic TREE drawing, (Color Plate 24), we find a simpler, more muted picture. The adjectives that stand out include alive, approachable, (somewhat) blooming, gentle, (somewhat) lonely, peaceful, (somewhat) sad, (somewhat) strong, and (somewhat) weak. The faint coloration of the leaf area and the inner branches promotes this mixed reaction.

Structurally, the BL area has none of the aggression and intricacy of the achromatic drawing. Its size, balance, and containment within the page convey a strong sense of adequacy in interacting with the environment. Yet the faint color gives the feeling of hesitancy and uncertainty.

Again, C. N. seems to relax when given an opportunity for affective expression and to permit himself to reveal the anxiety and uncertainty he experiences in reaching out for selfobject connectedness.

The heavy brown trunk lines again suggest the tension he experiences in maintaining his stance-in-the-world. The faint inner branches and knothole provide a sense of a lessening of tension with regard to dealing with personal interactive issues and traumas.

On the other hand, the heavy green line of grass at the bottom of the trunk conveys a feeling of a barrier to delving into the deeper underlying aspects of experience.

C. N.'s responses to the inquiry reveal a more centered sense of self when relating on a more expansive affective level. (The chromatic TREE is "30 to 40 years old, alive, and in the summer.") However, the "smiley-faced" sun in the upper left-hand corner, though hardly visible, evokes a sense of C. N.'s child-like affective experience of the presence of the powerful, life-giving source (again, mother?) in his world, even when focusing predominantly on a self-representation.

C. N. drew the FEMALE first when asked to draw a person (Figure 9.3), connoting the importance, subjectively, of the female selfobject in his life. The pencil FEMALE is also consid-

erably taller than the achromatic MALE (Figure 9.4). C. N.'s anxiety about his status as a male is thus revealed with feelings of inadequacy and a passive-submissive orientation vis-a-vis the female selfobject. The FEMALE's age, 30, relates the figure to his girlfriend or his ex-wife.

Impressionistically, the achromatic FE-MALE looks alive, alert, approachable, calm, (possibly) friendly, homely, open, and vigilant. The figure appears to be mild and unassuming, but conveying an enigmatic quality because of the intensity of the eyes, "Mona Lisa" smile, and wildish hairdo.

Beginning the structural analysis by examining the head, we are struck by its overly large size which conveys C. N.'s perception of the female selfobject as being overly-concerned with intellect, with a tendency to overcompensate for anxiety about her cognitive skills. This conforms to his description of both the exwife and the girlfriend. The overly large eyes, highlighted by the

FIGURE 9.3

heavy line quality, are the outstanding feature in the drawing. C. N. seems to be saying, "She is ever-alert, ever-vigilant, sees all." Relating to the female selfobject in the "real" world means feeling yourself to be under the intense, relentless scrutiny of a suspicious, possibly paranoid person.

In contrast, the ears, although heavily drawn, are much smaller than the other facial features and appear to be unattached and set out from the head. This may indicate C. N.'s perception of the female selfobject as capable of only selectively being able to "hear" him.

C. N. states that the achromatic FEMALE is "30, standing, posing for this picture, waiting to be able to move." She feels "excellent" and is thinking that "I feel pretty good, I feel accomplished." How do these responses jibe with the structural analysis depicting a paranoidal, over intellectual figure? Possibly, C. N. is reflecting his basic "real life" experience of the important women in his life, i.e., they may act in a compliant manner (posing, waiting), but they are essentially narcissistic and concerned with their own accomplishments.

The expression of the mouth elicits a sense of strain, of a forced pleasantness, an attempt to overcompensate for anxiety about interacting by appearing to be eager to engage.

The rather informal and "free" appearance of the hair is out-of-step with the less-than-sexy overall look of the figure. C. N. may be expressing a feeling that he experiences the female as suggesting a quality of sexual interest that she downplays in actual behavior. Following this, the FEMALE's neck is drawn as overly wide conveying the sense of someone who may have difficulty integrating thoughts and behavior and who may be given to impulsive outbursts.

The contradictory message may also be seen in the hint of cleavage but the barest outline of breasts.

Only the heavy outlining of the hands and fingers stands out when considering the rest of the drawing. C. N. may be depicting his anxiety about the female's ability to exert control of both her own and his life. The failure to draw wrist lines for the dress highlights C. N.'s anxiety about her faulty judgment and impulsive potential.

Drawing the figure with its feet touching the base of the page conveys C. N.'s perception of the the female as having feelings of insecurity and of needing support.

C. N. presents the female as lacking self-cohesion. Coupled with the relatively immobile position, the sense is of someone who is relatively constricted affectively and who emphasizes cognition and intellect over active involvement.

C. N.'s chromatic FEMALE, (Color Plate 25), in contrast, is not out-of-balance. When drawn with crayons, i.e., when given the opportunity to express a greater range of feelings than permitted by the pencil, this figure impresses as alive, alert, (somewhat) anxious, awkward, constricted, dreamy, meek, mild, quiet, reflective, tense, unthreatening, and young. Adopting the expression and stance of the figure, i.e., looking off to one side and holding one's arms in the angle depicted, helps to elicit much of this impression.

Structurally, the figure's eyes are heavily outlined indicating anxiety about receiving and reacting to affective stimuli. However, the impression is not the piercing, hypersensitive one of the pencil drawing but a much softer, easier to relate to image. The hair is more contained and the neck, while reinforced, is of moderate size. Thus, it is not the female's thoughts and fantasies that preoccupy C. N. when relating to her affectively; it is her difficulty taking on responsibility as seen in the sloping right shoulder and in her ability to carry out intentions and to reach out and make contact, as depicted in the awkward, stilted position of the arms, particularly the left one. Again, assuming the position of the figure, one feels the strain, the sense of being held back, and unable to freely connect with the environment.

No breasts are outlined for this picture conveying C. N.'s feeling that he does not experience the female as a nurturant or sexually mature figure.

The heavy black outline of the lower area of the body furthers the sense of C. N.'s preoccupation and distress with regard to the female selfobject's sexuality. It is as if this area were sectioned off as separate from his otherwise milder affective reaction to the figure. The squiggly red lines within the area may symbolize the intermittent, confused sexual interaction with the female.

The crayon female does not need the support of the bottom of the page but she has barely differentiated oval-shaped feet, which convey a sense of child-like immaturity and restricted autonomy.

Giving the chromatic figure an age of 36, which is more than five years older than either C. N.'s or his girlfriend's or exwife's true age, suggests a tendency to compensate for the anxiety he feels about her perceived immaturity. He states that the figure is alert to her surroundings but has to "leave, to get moving, to stop standing around." In this, C. N. may be expressing his dissatisfaction with her passivity. He sees her as "a little concerned, paranoid, anxious. She does not like the way she has been drawn." He seems to be aware, when relating with a greater range of affect, of her dissatisfaction with his criticality.

Turning to C. N.'s depiction of the MALE figure, the achromatic MALE (Figure 9.4) is openly identified as a self-portrait. The impressionistic analysis highlights these features: alive, alert, approachable, (somewhat) dependent, friendly, happy, informal, lively, open, pleasant, warm, and watchful. Although the impression is mostly favorable, there is an intensity to the facial expression that seems forced and pressured.

FIGURE 9.4

In many ways, this impression seems to be borne out in the structural analysis. The heavily drawn facial features draw our attention to C. N.'s tension with regard to his appearance, in general, and to his particular capacity to receive and react to affective stimuli and to interact with others. When relating to the "real," here-and-now world, C. N. elicits a sense of hypervigilance and guardedness. The overly large nose suggests an overly assertive compensation and the heavily drawn teeth convey aggressiveness behind the smile. The somewhat oversized head reveals the greater significance C. N. places on intellect over activity, but the discrepancy is felt to be much smaller for himself than for the female selfobject.

Partially concealing one arm behind the lightpole, points to some evasiveness or ambivalence about connecting with the environment. The heavily drawn right hand and overly large left suggest anxiety about being able to achieve control with a tendency to compensate by being overly active or assertive (similar to the overly large nose).

Some reinforcement around the crotch conveys C. N.'s sexual concerns. The drawn-over foot betrays avoidant anxiety with reference to achieving relative autonomy.

The placement of the figure toward the left side of the page elicits the feeling that C. N. may feel unable to move away from an early, dependent state of self-selfobject relatedness. His stance of leaning on the "source of light" (mother?) adds to the sense of C. N.'s dependent connection with a source of selfobject support. His answer to the question concerning what the figure is doing and thinking, i.e., "Waving to people, watching from a corner, and people watching. Hoping someone will wave back. Does not want to be standing by this pole all day, does not want the pole to be his only companion today," appears to attest to his awareness of and frustration with his dependent status. Furthering this, with regard to how the figure feels, he states, "Pretty good, not great, would like to be a little more aggressive and leave the pole and mix with the crowd."

Contrasting with the friendly but hypersensitive and hesitant figure conveyed by the achromatic drawing, C. N.'s chromatic MALE, (Color Plate 26), impresses as a "macho stud." The adjectives that correspond to this figure include (somewhat) aggressive, alive, assertive, assured, capable, confident, free, (somewhat) haughty, informal, self-centered, strong, tense, and watchful.

Again, the head is proportionately larger than the rest of the body pointing to the relative importance C. N. places on cognitive activity. However, the outstanding feature, structurally, is the size and heavy line quality and shading of the eyes. The inquiry reveals C. N.'s identification with the figure because of the green eye color and his awareness of the intensity with which he used this color. Although this is the color of his eyes in reality, the excessive use may indicate a wish to shore up uncertain self-esteem by overly assertive, grandiose-exhibitionistic compensatory behavior. This conforms to the impression of the figure as a somewhat haughty, confident figure. Anxiety about the ability to affectively interact with sources of selfobject gratification, (i.e., the heavy black, somewhat crooked mouth), contradicts the overall impression and replaces the "smiling but aggressive" mouth of the achromatic figure. C. N.'s anxiety about his sexual desirability is also revealed by the heavy shading of the hair.

The contrast between the achromatic and chromatic MALE figures seems to chart C. N.'s more dependent, less confident, more eager to please stance in the immediately interactive world versus a wish to be younger, more carefree and colorful, and more independent and individualistic when given the opportunity to relate on a wider band of affective interaction. Nevertheless, his anxiety and uncertainty about being able to "pull this off" and his self-criticality are reflected by his inquiry responses: the figure is about to "put his hands in his back pockets and take in a deep breath"; he is thinking, "who dressed me in this combination of clothes"; and he feels "very uncomfortable in his clothing and body." The lower page placement and reinforced grounding confirm a sense of felt insecurity.

Completing the analysis of the initial set of PDs, we turn to C. N.'s ANIMAL drawings. For the achromatic figure (Figure 9.5), C. N. drew a kangaroo. It impresses as active, affectionate, alert, alive, approachable, calm, friendly, kind, mild, peaceful, solid, soothing, warm, and young. It seems to be reaching out and eager to make contact.

Structurally, the reinforced pupil of the eye elicits a penetrating, hyperalert, but not suspicious sense of watchfulness. The figure may be reaching out, but is very watchful of what response it may get.

The apparent reduction of the ears to a more "normal" kangaroo size and the pleasant expression of the mouth, convey a more optimal sense of reacting to and interacting with the world.

FIGURE 9.5

Thus, when expressing more primitive aspects of the self in the here-and-now environment, C. N. seems to present a less guarded and tense picture than that given by the human figures.

The overly large size of the figure coupled with the somewhat dark line quality of the torso and limbs suggest a degree of overcompensation for tension with regard to C. N.'s sense of self-adequacy. However, the figure seems to be well-balanced suggesting a good degree of self-cohesion with reference to primitive affective and behavioral aspects of experience. Its reaching out position gives the feeling of an optimally active, assertive, interactive potential.

The type of animal chosen, a kangaroo, is rather uncommon.

The associations may range from nonassertive and maternal to pugnacious. This kangaroo looks quite friendly and nonaggressive. Its age, (two-and-a-half years), places it in the "young" category and suggests that C. N., when relating to others in the context of his more primal needs, has a lessened sense of felt maturity, perhaps a heightened sense of vulnerability.

Turning to the chromatic ANIMAL (Color Plate 27), a cat, the following adjectives stand out: alive, easy-going, lonely, meek, mild, passive, reflective, sad, shy, (somewhat) silly, and submissive. This cat looks like the opposite of Garfield, the brash, self-centered, "wise guy" of the cartoon strip. This one seems to be leaning forward to be petted, but is too shy to make eye contact or reveal any more direct request for involvement.

The heavy outlining of the facial features and the large size and dominant position of the head point to C. N.'s underlying anxiety about relating to others on an affective level. He may tend to compensate by making himself too available, too helpful without being able to directly express his deeper affective needs. The muted shading of the body and limbs attests to the uncertainty and hesitancy he feels about his strength and ability to connect with, control, and maneuver in the environment.

The good sense of self-cohesion, present in the achromatic ANIMAL, is not found in the chromatic drawing. C. N. may feel quite self-conscious when experiencing primitive selfobject needs and try to mask his discomfort by adopting a comical pose. Nevertheless, drawing a cat evokes the feeling of the desire to normalize his primitive needs and present them in an acceptable manner. The age given, 5, adds to the feeling that this presentation is more comparable to C. N.'s true sense of his felt level of maturity.

What, then, does the set of PDs completed at the outset of psychotherapy tell us about C. N.'s self-structure and selfobject relatedness?

To begin with, the consistent degree of care, effort, and attention to detail that characterize the achromatic drawings convey the sense of how involved with immediate selfobject surroundings C. N. is. There is no sense of a *"vertical split"* in which the side that relates to the day-to-day world is depleted—passive and enervated. Rather, C. N. strives to gain recognition and approval in the here-and-now, "real" world. His achromatic HOUSE reveals a person who attempts to do "too much," i.e., present himself as accessible, approachable, and related, while also emphasizing his superordinate preoccupation with warm familial involvement. The result is a feeling of being weighted down with concomitant fears of loss of control, insecurity, and lapses in judgment. Defensive and compensatory structures involving compulsivity and exhibitionism predominate.

The achromatic TREE revealed more of C. N.'s overstriving compensatory tendencies with reference to his anxiety about relating to others. Underlying this fear is his sense of insufficiency, of having little to offer. Hostile-aggressive tendencies were revealed as well as both a desire to reach beyond the limits of his environment and to close off from it.

The dominance of the female selfobject in C. N.'s life was evidenced by the achromatic FEMALE drawing. He depicts this figure as hypervigilant, much more involved with her cognitive activity than her behavioral, particularly sexual, potential. He presents the female as an enigmatic figure lacking in cohesiveness. She is depicted with both a passive-compliant and a narcissistic, impulsive side.

C. N.'s achromatic MALE figure, much smaller than the FEMALE, reveals, (like the achromatic HOUSE), his desire to relate freely to others on the one hand, but also his feelings of passive dependence on a source of support, on the other. Again, defensive hypersensitivity and compensatory overinvolvement and assertiveness are found.

Only when expressing his more primitive selfobject needs, in his achromatic drawing of an ANIMAL, does C. N. appear to present a less guarded and more openly vulnerable picture of himself. Yet, on this level, he seems to be capable of more directly reaching out for contact.

The value of acquiring both achromatic and chromatic drawings is demonstrated by the contrast between C. N.'s two sets of drawings.

The obsessive-compulsive quality of the pencil drawings gives way to a simpler, softer, more easy-going picture when C. N. has recourse to a wider range of affective expression. We find a more regressive, openly vulnerable, less eager to make contact side of his personality.

The chromatic HOUSE conveyed uncertainty about being accessible and approachable. He is not as related or connected to the environment. He is anxious about being able to maintain control and less eager to reveal himself. Nevertheless, the colors convey a sense of aliveness and vitality. When relieved of "reality" pressures, his focus is more inward than other related.

The chromatic TREE follows in this direction. There is a decidedly gentler, simpler, more sad-lonely, less aggressive, more peaceful feel to this drawing than the achromatic one. He is anxious about making contact and maintaining his position in the world.

C. N. also relaxes his depiction of the female selfobject when drawing her in color. He conveys her anxiety, tension, constrictedness, and sexual immaturity but also her mild, reflective, unthreatening side. She is more childlike and less intellectualized, enigmatic, and hypervigilant than the female he experiences in the here-and-now, less affectively nuanced world. He is more revealing of the conflictual aspects of his relationship with this figure.

In contrast to the FEMALE drawings, and the achromatic MALE drawing, C. N. presents a self-image in the chromatic MALE drawing that is more expansive. This drawing reflects his wish to express underlying grandiose-exhibitionistic yearnings. However, he cannot prevent the emergence of anxiety with concomitant hypervigilance with regard to how others will accept such an overt stance. He also reveals overly assertive compensatory behavior along with self-criticality and felt insecurity.

When given the opportunity to express primitive aspects of self on a broader affective continuum, C. N.'s chromatic ANIMAL more directly reveals the shy, passive, sad, and lonely side of himself. He seems to be revealing his desire for acceptance despite a sense of inadequacy and lack of cohesion.

Turning now to C. N.'s second set of PDs, done after he had completed one year of psychotherapy, we find considerable change in both the achromatic and chromatic drawings.

Beginning with the achromatic HOUSE (Figure 9.6), the impressionistic analysis yields a sense of looseness and lack of intensity that was absent in the first pencil HOUSE drawing (Figure 9.1). It impresses as (somewhat) accessible, approachable, (somewhat) friendly, informal, lived-in, modest, open, peaceful, and (somewhat) warm. C. N. appeared to put

FIGURE 9.6

more effort into the first drawing but crowded too much in. The second HOUSE has a more open but less precise feel. Instead of a huge chimney on the secondary wall we find a door. This enhances the sense that C. N. is now more involved with the ability to come and go in contrast to his involvement with what was happening inside the home.

Opening the structural analysis with an examination of the door on the main wall, one gets a sense of uncertainty and ambivalence about letting others in. The large portico suggests an attempt to appear more accessible than C. N. really feels capable or desirous of, as suggested by the smaller part that opens and the lack of connection with the baseline. The line quality ranges from dark to hasty-sketchy, conveying tension and indecision.

C. N. spends seemingly more effort on the door on the side wall. Here, the actual opening part is much larger than on the front wall. It has a more substantial feel. However, it is not connected to the baseline or a walkway; the position of the two windows in it can be seen as two eyes and it is facing towards the right, i.e., the part that lies ahead. All this can be said to add up to C. N.'s stronger involvement with his ability to pick-and-choose whom he makes himself available to than to his "public personna."

The difference from the first to the second pencil HOUSE drawings in how C. N. presents the windows follows this interpretation. From four elaborately detailed windows he draws two bare windows. The size of these windows conveys a feeling of openness, but the lack of details gives a sense of emptiness, of not revealing anything related to what is happening on the inside. The sketchy line quality carries along the sense of hesitancy about relating to the outside world. In contrast, the window on the side wall has a heavily reinforced window box. It's bent-over position seems to be saying, "Here is what I am offering you." The heavy line quality suggests that C. N. has a great deal of tension in making himself available on a selective basis, for relatedness to others.

With regard to the baseline and grounding, the latter has a hurried, scribbled quality while the former is quite faint. Although the HOUSE seems solidly based, these findings plus some transparency (including the outside portico walls), elicit a feeling of insecurity and anxiety about C. N.'s sense of felt stability.

The wall lines give a mixed feeling of relative solidity on the left, toward hesitancy on the right main wall, to tension and insecurity on the right side wall. Also, the size of the walls seems to diminish as it goes from left to right. Following the interpretations relating to the door and windows, C. N. may have greater anxiety about his sense of self-control in the context of contemplating greater connectedness to others in the future.

The size of the roof appears to be proportionately overly large. This is consistent with C. N. being more concerned with his inner thoughts and fantasies than at the beginning of therapy. The windows in the roof are drawn sketchily, quite unlike the sharply defined pair of the first achromatic HOUSE. Again, the sense is less one of "eyes" that are carefully observing the environment and more one of a "dreamy" kind of cursory viewing. The somewhat faint line quality of the roof is also in stark contrast to the clearly defined quality of the first HOUSE. While more preoccupied with inner cognitive process, C. N. seems vaguer, less certain than he appeared at the beginning of therapy.

When we consider the chimney and smoke, we find outstanding changes between the two drawings. The second chimney is quite small in relation to the roof but it has ample smoke coming out of it. C. N. apparently still has anxiety about warm familial involvement but no longer compensates by broadcasting his concerns. However, the profusion of smoke suggests that he experiences considerable self-selfobject involvement within the family.

Of note is the inclusion of a tree and the sun in the second achromatic HOUSE drawing. Unlike the colorful tree in Color Plate 23, this tree is on the left side, is rather phallic-looking, and virtually overhangs the HOUSE. The trunk is heavily drawn but the BL area is faint and sketchy. (There is also some transparency of the BL area and the roof.) The sun is on the right side and is heavily drawn and barren looking. Speculatively, the tree may represent the therapist, a significant selfobject who is experienced as powerful, with whom interrelating is uncertain but who "penetrates" C. N.'s inner thoughts and fantasies. The sun may represent the maternal selfobject whose omnipresence is anxiety provoking and who offers little warmth.

C. N.'s responses to the inquiry focus on a selfobject milieu that can bring the warmth and security he craves. "A family, their children and pets," live in the HOUSE. It is "warm, secure, safe, comfortable."

It appears then, that after a year of therapy, C. N. relates in the here-and-now selfobject world of home and family with a greater experience of warmth. He appears to be less compensatory, more openly uncertain and private, but with a view toward greater interaction with others in the future.

When we examine the second chromatic HOUSE (Color Plate 28), we are impressed by its size and substantiality. It appears to be accessible, approachable, attractive, comfortable, friendly, good-looking, lived-in, open, organized, peaceful, pleasant, stable, solid, strong, warm, and well-planned. It seems like the "grown-up" version of C. N.'s first chromatic HOUSE (Color Plate 23).

Now, when afforded the opportunity to relate with a greater range of affect, C. N. reveals an "up-front" quality that was not present the previous year and that is still difficult for him on a limited black-and-white basis.

While he conveys a strong sense of accessibility, he is circumspect about how approachable he is and how interrelated he wishes to be on the "ground" level. (There is no walkway and the lower windows are bare or guarded by shrubs.) The greater differentiation of the second floor windows elicits the impression that C. N. needs to have a greater sense of distance or control before he will become more fully related to others. The heavily drawn red flower box conveys his anxiety about relating in a more intense, exciting way.

The sketchy, somewhat heavy quality of the wall lines suggests that he is still somewhat tense and uncertain about maintaining self-control. The relative straightness of the left wall line versus the broken quality of the right, (coupled with the expansiveness of the window on the left versus the crowding on the right), point to C. N.'s having shored up his past but being uncertain, with a feeling of less control about what is yet to come.

In line with this we have a strong looking roof but with a line quality that is smooth and even on the left side but heavier and more broken on the right.

Additionally, the substantial, nicely bricked-in chimney with ample smoke, completes the picture of C. N. having resolved many issues concerning the warm relationships he and his important selfobjects are capable of. Drawing the chimney in brown, rather than the customary red, highlights C. N.'s concern with security in this area.

The heavily shaded sun on the far right side suggests that relationships with mother bode problematic in the future. The proportionately smaller tree on the left side may indicate that while the therapist looms large in the "real" world, his importance is less powerful and intrusive and more contained with regard to C. N.'s affective self-state and involvements.

C. N.'s response that "a man and his wife and their children" live in the house and it is "very comfortable, just the right size to be safe and warm," points to his greater capacity, affectively, to assume responsibility for his significant involvements and to find peace and security. During the year, C. N. strengthened his relationship with his girlfriend, they got married, and were awaiting the birth of a child.

What a contrast we find when we compare the second achromatic TREE drawing (Figure 9.7) with the first (Figure 9.2). The former gives the impression of being hastily dashed-off compared to the intricate care taken with the latter. The second TREE could be alive or dead; it seems to be barren, cold, gloomy, odd, and symmetrical. If the top is seen as the head of a human body, its inner design conveys a feeling of "sad eyes."

Structurally, the BL area is proportionately large. C. N. may be expressing his ongoing concern with having to spend too much time and effort interacting with the "real" world. The stylized manner in which he drew the outline and the generally faint line quality (except for the uppermost portion) convey the sense that over the course of the year, he has disengaged from the complex hyper-involvement he felt was necessary to interact and adopted a more stereotyped, essentially removed kind of interaction. The heavier line quality of the top section elicits the impression that he is more guarded and experiences greater tension in the area that corresponds to thoughts and feelings.

FIGURE 9.7

The inner details are shaped like "Vs," sharply pointing downward to a phallic-shaped "U." It may be speculated that C. N. is focused, inwardly, on his sexual capability, his need to "act like a man" given his new status as husband and father.

The penetrated and scribbled right trunk line conveys C. N.'s anxiety about his strength for what lies ahead.

The lack of roots or grounding furthers the sense of C. N.'s insecurity about his being grounded in the here-and-now world and his lack of connection with his inner self.

C. N.'s description of the TREE as 15 years old, alive, and in the season of winter, attests to his lessened sense of felt maturity and a feeling of barrenness.

When we compare this rather gloomy self-picture to that given by the second chromatic TREE (Color Plate 29), we are again struck by how C. N. now responds to the opportunity for affective expression with an expanded burst of vitality. In contrast to the second achromatic TREE but also to the first chromatic one (Color Plate 24), this TREE gives the impression of being alive, approachable, blooming, cheerful, colorful, healthy, inviting, lively, and wholesome. Like the chromatic HOUSE (Color Plate 28), however, the more lively impression given by the capacity to express himself affectively, reveals, upon structural analysis, problematic issues that need to be addressed.

The BL area is drawn somewhat more heavily on the left side eliciting a sense of C. N. wanting to block off the past. The "busyness" of the left side gives way to a more open feeling on the right, suggesting a movement from hyperactivity to a more open, expanding kind of interaction with the environment.

The heavy red of the fruit may correspond to C. N.'s anxiety about his fecundity but in the context of joy and excitement.

The lighter line quality of the trunk suggests C. N.'s uncertainty about his ability to find the strength within to support the fruit-bearing part (as the two branches ascending into the BL area give the impression of doing). The scribbled inner lines further the sense of inner anxiety. The trunk's widening from the base to where it joins the BL area adds to the feeling of C. N.'s tendency to compensate by inflating his sense of capability for the underlying anxiety about his adequacy.

Although the TREE conveys some feeling of felt stability, it appears to be much less grounded than the first chromatic TREE. What C. N. may have given up in a feeling of stability, he may have gained in a sense of expansiveness.

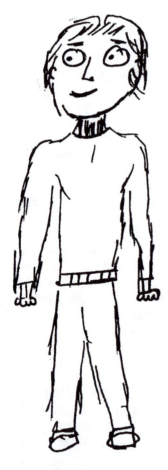

Not drawing the roots evokes a sense of C. N. not attending to deeper self issues, but there is not the "barrier" found in the first drawing. Nor is the sun included as in the first drawing. None of these indications of C. N.'s anxiety about his self-state overshadow the overall awareness, on an affective level, of a more definite, alive sense of self compared to when he began therapy. The inquiry, in which he responds that the TREE is "Thirty years, very alive, thriving, and in spring/summer," attests to that interpretation.

The first reaction to C. N.'s human figure drawings is to the fact that he drew the achromatic MALE first in the set done after one year (Figure 9.8). This figure is also slightly taller than the second achromatic FEMALE (Figure 9.9). This seems to attest to the greater security that he achieved during the year in his status as a male and his sense of an optimal capacity to assert himself vis-a-vis the female.

Figure 9.8 gives the impression of being alive, alert, calm, friendly, intelligent, pleasant, reflective, and (somewhat) weak. He seems to be watching something in a rather benign way but still feeling somewhat tense.

FIGURE 9.8

Structurally, the figure's head is proportionately larger than the body, again conveying the relative importance C. N. places on intellect over behavior. The relatively moderate line quality of the facial features as compared to the first achromatic MALE, gives an impression of much less tension with regard to receiving and reacting to affective stimuli. The eyes are quite large, however, pointing to C. N.'s continued hyper-awareness of the environment but without the intensity of the previous year. The ears are small but reinforced so as to be sure to be seen. C. N. may be less concerned with what is said, but wants to make sure that you know he is listening. The mouth is reinforced suggesting some tension about affective interaction, but the slightly smiling expression is much more relaxed than the toothy grin of the previous year. This gives the feeling that he no longer overcompensates for anxiety about relating by being "too friendly."

C. N. heavily reinforces the neck, suggesting anxiety about modulating his thoughts and actions, but the moderate size of the neck strengthens the sense that he feels basically capable of such control.

The drawing of the right side of the figure (left side of the drawing) is markedly different from the left. The right shoulder is more distinct than the left, and the right arm is thicker than the left and has a more pressured line quality. There is also erasure of the right arm. This seems to be a reflection of C. N.'s anxiety and subsequent ambivalence about his ability to shoulder responsibility and meaningfully connect with the environment. There is a sense of adequacy offset by uncertainty and felt weakness. The tiny, reinforced hands on both sides convey a general sense of felt inability to exert control and a tight, inhibited self-experience.

The overly long trunk, (in comparison to the legs), points to overcompensation for the felt lack of strength by "stretching himself too thin," i.e., taking on too much.

The somewhat reinforced belt coupled with the faint genital line suggest uncertainty and tension with regard to sexual capability.

The small hips and short legs give a feeling of inchoateness and passivity about confidently maneuvering in the world.

The reinforced feet add a sense of tension about C. N.'s feeling of being able to adopt a relatively autonomous stance.

In the here-and-now world, C. N. appears to lack a strong sense of cohesiveness and balance. His inquiry responses feature "thinking and pondering" about the "meaning of a statue." Can he be pondering his own capacity to "come alive" versus remaining immobile? Consciously, C. N. states that the figure is "very content with his ideas and thoughts." Possibly, in contrast to his hypersensitivity and need to make contact of the previous year, as well as the elimination of his dependence on the "source of light," C. N. feels more centered in his greater emphasis on self. This relates to the positive first impression obtained in first perusing the drawing.

C. N.'s second chromatic MALE drawing (Color Plate 30) again stands in stark contrast to his chromatic MALE of the previous year (Color Plate 26). "Mr. Macho" is now a passive, friendly, boyish-looking young man. He impresses as being alert, approachable, fragmented, happy, (somewhat) inadequate, and (somewhat) stiff. He appears to be very interested in something, but rigidly stuck in his place with no indication that he is capable of moving towards it.

Here, given greater affective freedom, C. N. draws the head in a more stylized way, not drawing an outline to contain the features. This may indicate both the wish for and the fear of greater freedom to transcend conventional boundaries in relating to the environment. The relative largeness of the head again points to C. N.'s greater involvement in thinking and fantasizing than in action. The heavily reinforced circular eyes elicit a sense of single-minded intensity as opposed to the hypervigilance of the drawings done at the beginning of therapy. These eyes look like "burning coals" that belie the otherwise happy expression.

Coupled with the omission of ears, the eyes may indicate an inwardness of focus that C. N. feels free now to openly reveal.

The fact that the neck is attached to the body, but not to the head, points to the felt unavailability of cognitive resources that could control impulsive behavior. The lack of an outline for the head may then suggest that C. N. is experiencing previously repressed fantasies. This may account for the stiffness and rigid immobility of the figure which he self-imposes in order not to act out.

The short arms, tiny hands, and relatively short, immobilized legs, and small feet all point to a sense of restricted capacity to connect with, control, and maneuver in the world. The feet touching the base of the page and the reinforced grounding convey C. N.'s sense of insecurity and his need for support at this time. Nevertheless, the substantial torso gives an indication of C. N.'s basic sense of inner strength. The relatively subdued colors attest to the uncertainty with which he feels he can manifest this strength, however.

C. N.'s responses to the inquiry appear to belie any conscious preoccupation with threatening ideas. ("Watching people in a park. Thinking what a beautiful day it is. Feels great.") However, giving the figure the age of 21 may attest to his lessened sense of maturity and greater propensity for regressive behavior.

The second achromatic FEMALE (Figure 9.9) looks like a little girl who is dressed like an old lady. This impression is augmented by these adjectives: alert, friendly, passive, and simple. She stands in stark contrast to the first achromatic FEMALE (Color Plate 24) with the piercing gaze, enigmatic smile, and reinforced hands.

Structurally, the circular outline of the head suggests that C. N. now simplifies and closes off the part of the female that thinks about and responds to the world in contrast to the differentiation and openness of the previous year. The heavy line quality of the head in contrast to the rest of the body, suggests that C. N. is more concerned with how this figure thinks than in how she behaves. He presents her as severely restricted in her ability to receive or convey affective impressions. She is smiling but the heavy reinforcement of the mouth indicates anxiety about interacting with others. The hair is added on in such a way as to convey no real involvement with sexual thoughts or fantasies or with concern for being attractive to others.

FIGURE 9.9

The body is drawn so as to minimize her ability to shoulder responsibility, connect with or maneuver in the environment. The proportionately large feet, in contrast, do give a sense of someone who overemphasizes her ability to stand on her own.

C. N. responds to the inquiry that the figure is 11 years old, "getting ready for bed, saying good night, feeling safe in her home (and) very happy." This description seems to emphasize a movement away from the world into the security of the home.

The overall sense is that C. N. has made a major shift in his experience of the female selfobject from a striving, hypervigilant achiever to a more passive, inwardly oriented figure. Although he is concerned about what she may be thinking, he seems to be content to experience her as less sexual and active in the here-and-now world. All this is consistent with C. N.'s concern with his wife as a mother-to-be, her adequacy to fulfill this role, and his need to provide support for both her and the baby.

The second chromatic FEMALE (Color Plate 31), is also drawn as a little girl. There is more consistency between the second achromatic and chromatic FEMALE figures than those drawn at the beginning of therapy. However, given greater affective freedom, C. N. draws this little girl as being more open to the world. Yet, her face has a mask-like appearance.

The adjectives that spring to mind when reacting to her open-armed pose—approachable, friendly, trusting, and warm—all become questionable when considering the stereotypical facial features. The pose seems to be saying, "Here I am, let's hug," but the face is more inscrutable.

Similar to the achromatic figure, the facial features, structurally, convey restrictedness and anxiety about interacting with others. However, the blending of the hair with the head suggests greater readiness to experience her as a sexually cognizant person. The rather large, reinforced chin indicates concern about her being too assertive. When C. N. can let his feelings out, his underlying fear of her perceived tendency to overcompensate for passivity emerges.

The lack of a neck adds to the perception of her potential for impulsivity but the short arms, small hands, and rigidly connected legs all evoke a sense of the figure's minimal potential for acting-out. The blue color also conveys a sense of calm and peace that belies a more active, aggressive approach to the environment.

Thus, given greater affective range, C. N. seems to give expression to his experience of the female selfobject as more responsive but also unpredictable and inscrutable. He is fearful of her impulsivity but sees her mainly as relatively restricted in her acting out potential. The responses to the inquiry confirm his perception of her as being both immature and more outgoing. ("She is six years old, saying hello, thinking how nice it is to be standing in front of people. She is very happy.")

What do we find from the second ANIMAL drawings? The chromatic cat, "Garfield?," (Color Plate 77) is now the achromatic ANIMAL figure (Figure 9.10), but here he is presented as cozily curled up on a mat. The impression is of peaceful contentment. Both impressionistically and structurally, the sense is of C. N.'s being at home with the more primitive aspect of his self structure with less need to reach out for contact as reflected in the first achromatic ANIMAL drawing (Figure 9.5), or shyly request it (as in the first chromatic drawing).

The heavily drawn lines suggest that C. N. is not quite at ease with this rather contented picture and needs to consciously reinforce it.

The parrot-like bird drawn as the second chromatic ANIMAL (Color Plate 32) has a rather dour expression compared to the pencil cat. When afforded the opportunity for greater affective range, C. N. appears to manifest the same pattern as revealed in the human figures, i.e., a wish to interact with the environment in an affectively free manner counteracted by a feeling of restriction, of being tied down. Here, this colorful, exotic bird is seated on a perch. He looks glumly off, the heavily drawn eye suggesting anxiety about relating, evoking a sense of defensive avoidance and withdrawal. The heavily drawn red tail conveys a feeling of anxiety about expressing his desire for intensity, excitement, and fulfillment, particularly with reference to primitive sexual impulses.

C. N. gives the bird the age of two years. In contrast to the cat's age of nine, this suggests a lessened sense of felt maturity when experiencing his primitive affective potential. The large size of the bird indicates the extent to which C. N. is invested in relating to these feelings.

FIGURE 9.10

C. N.'s two sets of PDs reveal a progression from how he experienced himself and his selfobject world when reacting on a here-and-now, black-and-white basis versus one which afforded a greater range of affective expression.

When he began therapy, each of the five pairs of drawings exhibited a similar pattern, i.e., the achromatic drawing was more detailed and intense while the chromatic drawing was simpler and softer. To a large degree, after a year in treatment, that pattern was reversed. C. N. seemed to have less need to deal with the immediate world in such a precise and defended manner, but was more revealing of both expansive and inward tendencies when provided with greater freedom of expression, affectively.

The value of obtaining the five different drawings was demonstrated in what each provided to our understanding of the patient's personality structure and the possible effects of life experience and psychotherapy on it. The latter focused on providing a mirroring experience for C. N.'s self-assertive potential, particularly with regard to expressing both positive and negative affect to the significant female selfobjects in his life.

The HOUSE drawings, which relate to the individual's connections to both the familial and environmental selfobject milieus, revealed a shift in which C. N. experienced more warmth within the home, less compensatory eagerness to connect with others, and greater anxiety about future interactions.

The TREE drawings, which reveal a comprehensive image of self-structure, displayed C. N.'s pulling back from expending so much effort in attempting to outwardly interact which drained him emotionally to a more superficial surface involvement but a more vivid, joyful affective experience in the world.

The MALE and FEMALE drawings, which relate to both self and selfobject conceptions, revealed a tremendous degree of change, particularly with regard to a reversal in feelings of assertiveness and independence vis-a-vis the female selfobject. C. N. appeared to be freer to reveal doubts about his ability to connect with, control, and maneuver in the environment, but he became considerably less hypervigilant and given to overcompensation for felt inadequacies. He also shifted a perception of the female as either a huge, frightening figure or a dreamy, distorted one to a more consistent conception of a nonsexual child who is less capable of functioning in the world and who, by inference, requires greater protection.

The ANIMAL drawings, which are involved with the expression of primitive needs and affects, completed the picture of a movement from a more overt appeal to others for selfobject gratification to a more inward, consciously content but affectively troubled awareness of frustrated need.

It was previously stated that C. N. made a tremendous transition in his life during the year from being confused and unsettled in his relationship with his girlfriend to being able to make a commitment to her. The drawings reveal the shift to a more self-reflective position and the anxiety which underlies this major life change. The anxiety, however, seems to be less involved with achieving immediate selfobject gratification and more with how he is going to deal with what lies ahead of him.

POSTSCRIPT

It was the aim of this book to provide a comprehensive guide for the clinician to utilize selected projective drawings to illuminate the therapeutic process by revealing changes in self-structure and self-selfobject relatedness. I hope that the empathically derived explanations and case examples that were provided have succeeded in encouraging the application of self psychological principles to the interpretation of projective drawings and their use in psychotherapy.

APPENDIX A

☐ Examiner Instructions

The following directions may be used when administering the Projective Drawing Test:

Place a pencil and piece of paper in front of the subject (*S*). (Paper should be 8½ x 11 inches, white, presented length-wise. Permit *S* to turn it any way (s)he wishes. Pencil should be #2, soft lead, with eraser.)

Say: *"I'd like you to do some drawings. This is not a test of your artistic ability so don't worry about your skill. Just take your time and try to do the best you can. First, draw a HOUSE; any HOUSE is O.K."*

If *S* asks, e.g., about turning the page, using any part of it or the whole page, including different features, etc., simply say, *"Whatever you like"* or a similar phrase. Do this for all subsequent drawings. If *S* questions the purpose of the test, reply that it is a method psychologists use to learn about someone's personality.

Prevent the use of a ruler or straight edge. Record *S's* remarks or actions in an unobtrusive way.

Remove each drawing as soon as *S* has finished, but permit additions or corrections if requested, making note of them. Allow a maximum of about five minutes for each drawing.

After the HOUSE is completed, present another page and say, *"Now, I'd like you to draw a TREE. Any kind of TREE is O.K."* For this and all succeeding drawings, add that *S* can take his/her time and should try to do their best.

Then ask *S* to draw *"A PERSON, a full-length, whole PERSON."* Prevent the drawing of a stick figure or head alone. Accept a drawing of a "partial" person, e.g., head and upper torso, or person with no legs.

Then say, *"Now draw a PERSON of the opposite sex from the one you just drew—a full-length, whole PERSON."* (Clarify confusion by saying, e.g., *"If you drew a male first, now draw a female."*)

Next, ask for a drawing of an ANIMAL, *"a whole animal."*

After the ANIMAL is completed, remove the pencil and the drawings, present a box of crayons (Crayola–8 crayon box). Say: *"Now I'd like you to do another set of drawings of a HOUSE, TREE, etc. using crayons only. You can draw the same or similar HOUSE, TREE, PERSONS, or ANIMAL or something entirely different. You can use as many or as few crayons as you like."*

Then proceed to administer the test exactly as with the pencil drawings.

After completion of the crayon drawings say, *"Now, I'd like to ask you some questions about your drawings."* Hold up the first drawing of the HOUSE and say, *"Who lives in this HOUSE?"* Record the answer verbatim on the **back** of the page. (Record responses to all subsequent drawings on the **back** also.) For a response which indicates that *S* alone or a single person lives in the HOUSE, inquire if anybody else lives there. If *S* has difficulty accepting the original concept, explain, e.g., *"If the HOUSE were real, who would be living in it?"* Then ask *"What kind of feeling does the HOUSE give you?"* (or *"What kind of feeling do you get from this HOUSE, e.g., warm or cold, comfortable or not, etc.?"* Record *S's* response as well as any spontaneous comments *S* adds for this as well as all succeeding drawings.

For the TREE, ask *"How old is this TREE?"* Press for a number rather than, e.g., "A young tree" or "very old," but accept whatever response is given. Next, ask *"Is it alive or dead?"* Then ask *"What season of the year is it in?"*

For the FIRST PERSON drawn, ask *"Did you have someone in mind when you drew this PERSON or does he/she remind you of anybody?"* If you cannot determine the sex of the PERSON, ask. Then ask *"How old is this PERSON?"* Then, *"What is the PERSON doing?"*; then, *"What is (s)he thinking?"*; then, *"How is (s)he feeling?"*

Follow the same procedure for the SECOND PERSON.

For the ANIMAL, ask what kind of ANIMAL it is; (write this on the **front** of the page). Then, ask how old it is; (record on the **back**).

Do this for all 10 drawings. If *S* draws the same things for the crayon drawings as for the pencil drawings and says all the answers are the same, read them aloud while copying them onto the color drawings. Record any additions or modifications.

Following administration and interrogation write *S's* name, date of birth, and date of testing on the back of each sheet and number each page on the upper right-hand corner of the front (1 to 5 for each set).

☐ Instructions for Self-Administration

It may not be possible to administer the Projective Drawing Test in person. Despite the obvious limitations of self-administration, the value of having this data for a given patient or client outweighs whatever losses ensue from not having direct observation of the process.

The following set of instructions (along with a #2, soft lead pencil, box of 8 Crayola crayons, and 10 sheets of white 8½ x 11" paper) should be provided to the patient.

☐ Instructions

1) Find a quiet place where you can work alone with no distractions. Do not show your drawings to anyone.
2) Do not use "models," e.g., pictures or objects in the room; draw from your imagination.
3) Use the pencil provided for the pencil drawings and use the box of crayons for the crayon drawings. Make one drawing per page. If you want to start over, use the other side of the page. Do not use a ruler or straight edge.
4) This is not a test of your artistic ability. Don't worry about your skill. Just try to do the best you can. Take your time but don't spend too much time on any one drawing. Try to finish all the drawings in one sitting. Make any changes or additions while you are drawing, but after you have finished, do not try to change or improve any of the drawings.
5) First, draw a HOUSE; any house is O.K. You can turn the page any way you want, erase, include whatever you want, etc. for this and all of the following drawings.
6) Take a new page. Draw a TREE; any kind of tree is O.K.
7) Take a new page. Draw a PERSON, a full-length, whole person. Do not draw a stick figure.
8) Take a new page. Draw a PERSON OF THE OPPOSITE SEX (or GENDER) from the one you just drew—a full-length, whole person.
9) Take a new page. Draw an ANIMAL, a whole animal; any kind of animal is O.K.
10) Put away the pencil and pencil drawings and, using only the crayons, repeat steps 5 to 9. Again, do one drawing to a page. You can draw the same or similar HOUSE, TREE, PERSONS, or ANIMAL or something entirely different. Do not copy your pencil drawings. Do not use the pencil at all. You may use as many or as few crayons as you like.

11) After completion of both the pencil and crayon drawings, answer the following questions. (Write your answers on the back of each of the respective 10 drawings.)

☐ Questions

House:

1) Who lives in this house?; (or, Who might live in this house if it were real?)
2) What kind of feeling do you get from this house, e.g., warm or cold, comfortable or not, etc.?; (or, What kind of feeling does this house give you?)

Tree:

1) How old is this tree? (Please give a number.)
2) Is it alive or dead?
3) What season of the year is it in?

First Person:

1) Did you have someone in mind when you drew this person or does he/she remind you of anybody?
2) What is the person's sex (or gender)?
3) How old is this person? (Please give a number.)
4) What is (s)he doing?
5) What is (s)he thinking?
6) How is (s)he feeling?

Second Person:

Answer questions (1) to (6) as with first person.

Animal:

1) What kind of animal is it?
2) How old is it? (Please give a number.)

When S returns the completed drawings, review each one and the answers to the questions and record any clarifications that are necessary.

APPENDIX B

☐ The Adjective Lists

House

ACCESSIBLE	CUTE	IMAGINATIVE	PRACTICAL	STRANGE
ALIVE	DEAD	IMMACULATE	PRECISE	STRONG
APPROACHABLE	DECORATIVE	INACCESSIBLE	PRETTY	STURDY
ARTISTIC	DEPRESSING	INFORMAL	PRIMITIVE	UNAFFECTED
ATTRACTIVE	DETAILED	INVENTIVE	QUEER	UNAPPROACH-
AUSTERE	DIFFERENT	LIVED-IN	RAM-	ABLE
BARREN	DIGNIFIED	MASCULINE	SHACKLE	UNASSUMING
BIZARRE	DILAPIDATED	MODERATE	RELATED	UNCONVENTIONAL
CHARMING	DISTORTED	MODEST	REMOTE	UNFRIENDLY
CHEERFUL	DULL	NATURAL	SAD	UNINHABITED
CLOSED-OFF	ELABORATE	NEW	SCARY	UNINVITING
CHILDISH	EMPTY	ODD	SEVERE	UNREALISTIC
COLD	EXHIBITIONISTIC	OLD	SIMPLE	UNSTABLE
COLORFUL	EXPANSIVE	OPEN	SKIMPY	UNUSUAL
COMFORTABLE	FABULOUS	ORDINARY	SLIPSHOD	WARM
COMPULSIVE	FEMININE	ORGANIZED	SNOBBISH	WEAK
CONFINING	FORMAL	ORIGINAL	SOCIABLE	WEALTHY
CONFUSING	FRIENDLY	OSTENTATIOUS	SOLID	WELL-
CONSERVATIVE	FRIGHTENING	OVER-	SOPHISTI-	PLANNED
CONVENTIONAL	FUSSY	POWERING	CATED	WHIMSICAL
COZY	GLOOMY	PEACEFUL	SPOOKY	WHOLESOME
CRAMPED	GUARDED	PECULIAR	STABLE	WEIRD
CREATIVE	HAPPY	PLEASANT	STATELY	WORN-DOWN
CRUDE	HOSTILE	POOR	STERILE	ZANY

Tree

AGGRESSIVE	DYING	PEACEFUL	UNUSUAL
ALIVE	ELABORATE	PECULIAR	WEAK
ALOOF	EXPANSIVE	PLEASANT	WHOLESOME
ANGRY	FEMININE	POWERFUL	WEIRD
APPROACHABLE	FRAGMENTED	PRECISE	WILD
ASSERTIVE	FRIGHTENING	PROTECTIVE	WITHDRAWN
ARTIFICIAL	GENTLE	QUEER	YOUNG
AWKWARD	HEALTHY	REALISTIC	
BALANCED	HOSTILE	RELIABLE	
BARREN	IMAGINATIVE	REMOVED	
BEAUTIFUL	IMMATURE	SAD	
BLOOMING	INVITING	SCARY	
BUSY	ISOLATED	SHELTERING	
CHARMING	LIVELY	SICK	
CHEERFUL	LONELY	SIMPLE	
COLD	MAGNIFICENT	SOLID	
COLORFUL	MASCULINE	SPARSE	
CONFUSING	MATURE	STARK	
CONSTRICTED	MODEST	STRONG	
CONVENTIONAL	NATURAL	SYMMETRICAL	
CUT-OFF	ODD	TIRED	
DEAD	OLD	TOUGH	
DETAILED	ORDINARY	UNASSUMING	
DISTORTED	ORIGINAL	UNCONVENTIONAL	
DIFFERENT	OVERFLOWING	UNDEVELOPED	
DISTANT	OVERPOWERING	UNREALISTIC	
DOMINATING	PATHETIC	UNSTEADY	

Male/Female

ACTIVE	CRAZY	IMMATURE	ORIGINAL	STIFF
ALIVE	CREATIVE	IMPULSIVE	OVERPOWERING	STRONG
AFRAID	CRUEL	INADEQUATE	PASSIVE	STUBBORN
AGGRESSIVE	DANGEROUS	INDEPENDENT	PEACEFUL	STUPID
ALERT	DEPENDENT	INDIFFERENT	PLEASANT	SUBMISSIVE
ANGRY	DEPRESSED	INFORMAL	POOR	SUSPICIOUS
ANXIOUS	DIGNIFIED	INTELLIGENT	PRETTY	SWEET
APPROACHABLE	DISTORTED	INVOLVED	PRISSY	TENSE
ASSERTIVE	DREAMY	KIND	PRUDISH	TRUSTING
ASSURED	DULL	LAZY	PROTECTIVE	UGLY
ATTRACTIVE	DYING	LIVELY	QUIET	UNIMAGIN-
AWKWARD	EFFEMINATE	LONELY	REALISTIC	ATIVE
BEAUTIFUL	FANTASTIC	LOOSE	REFINED	UNIQUE

BIZARRE	FEMININE	LOUD	REFLECTIVE	UNTHREAT-
CALM	FLIRTATIOUS	LOVING	RELAXED	ENING
CAPABLE	FORMAL	MACHO	RIGID	VIGILANT
CARING	FRAGMENTED	MASCULINE	SAD	WARM
CLOSED-OFF	FREE	MATURE	SANE	WATCHFUL
CLOWNISH	FRIENDLY	MEEK	SELF-	WITHDRAWN
COARSE	FRIGHTENING	MILD	CENTERED	WEALTHY
COLD	FRIVOLOUS	MODERATE	SERIOUS	WEAK
COMPLICATED	GOOD-LOOKING	NASTY	SEXY	YOUNG
CONCEITED	GROTESQUE	NORMAL	SICK	YOUTHFUL
CONFIDENT	HAPPY	OLD	SILLY	
CONFUSED	HAUGHTY	OPEN	SIMPLE	
CONSTRICTED	HEALTHY	ORDINARY	SOLID	

Animal

ACTIVE	DULL	LIVELY	SAD
AFFECTIONATE	DYING	LONELY	SICK
AGGRESSIVE	EASY-GOING	MASCULINE	SILLY
ALERT	FANTASTIC	MATURE	SERIOUS
ALIVE	FEARFUL	MEEK	SOLID
ANGRY	FEMININE	MILD	SOOTHING
APPROACHABLE	FEROCIOUS	MODERATE	STRONG
ASSERTIVE	FRAGMENTED	NASTY	STUBBORN
BEAUTIFUL	FREE	NATURAL	STUPID
BIZARRE	FRIENDLY	NERVOUS	SUBMISSIVE
CALM	FRIGHTENING	NORMAL	SUSPICIOUS
CAPABLE	FRIVOLOUS	OLD	TENSE
CARING	GOOD-LOOKING	ORDINARY	TIRED
CLOWNISH	GROTESQUE	ORIGINAL	TRUSTING
COARSE	HAPPY	OVERPOWERING	UNAPPROACHABLE
COLD	HAUGHTY	PASSIVE	UGLY
CONSTRICTED	HEALTHY	PEACEFUL	UNTHREATENING
CONFIDENT	HELPFUL	PECULIAR	UNUSUAL
CONFUSED	HOSTILE	PROTECTIVE	UNIQUE
COWARDLY	IMMATURE	PROUD	VICIOUS
CRUEL	INADEQUATE	QUIET	WARM
DANGEROUS	INDEPENDENT	REALISTIC	WEAK
DEAD	INDIFFERENT	REFINED	WISE
DEPENDENT	INTELLIGENT	RELAXED	WITHDRAWN
DEPRESSED	KIND	RIGID	YOUNG
DISTORTED	LAZY	RELIABLE	YOUTHFUL

REFERENCES

Anastasi, A. (1982). *Psychological testing* (5th ed.). New York: Macmillan.

Bacal, H. A., & Newman, K. M. (1990). *Theories of object relations: Bridges to self psychology* New York: Columbia University Press.

Basch, M. (1980). *Doing psychotherapy*. New York: Basic Books.

Bieliauskas, V. J. (1980). *The House-Tree-Person (H-T-P) research review: 1980 edition*. Los Angeles: Western Psychological Services.

Buck, J. N. (1948). The H-T-P technique, a qualitative and quantitative scoring manual. *Journal of Clinical Psychology, 4,* 317–396.

Buck, J. N. (1966). *The House-Tree-Person technique: Revised manual*. Los Angeles: Western Psychological Services.

Buck, J. N. (1992). *House-Tree-Person projective drawing technique: Manual and interpretive guide*. Revised by W. L. Warren. Los Angeles: Western Psychological Services.

Burns, R. C. (1982). *Self growth in families*. New York: Brunner/Mazel.

Burns, R. C. (1987). *Kinetic House-Tree-Person drawings: An interpretive manual*. New York: Brunner/Mazel.

Burns, R. C., & Kaufman, S. (1970). *Kinetic family drawings (K-F-D)*. New York: Brunner/Mazel.

Burns, R. C., & Kaufman, S. H. (1972). *Actions, styles and symbols in kinetic family drawings*. New York: Brunner/Mazel.

Chessick, R. D. (1985). *Psychology of the self and the treatment of narcissism*. New York: Jason Aronson.

DiLeo, J. H. (1970). *Young children and their drawings*. New York: Brunner/Mazel.

DiLeo, J. H. (1973). *Interpreting children's drawings*. New York: Brunner/Mazel.

Exner, J. E. (1993). *The Rorschach: A comprehensive system: Vol.1. Basic foundations (3rd ed.)*. New York: Wiley.

Farlyo, B., & Paludi, M. (1985). Research with the Draw-A-Person test: Conceptual and methodological issues. *The Journal of Abnormal Psychology, 119,* 575–580.

Gillespie, J. (1994). *The projective use of mother-and-child drawings*. New York: Brunner/Mazel.

Goldberg, A. (1995). *The problem of perversion*. New Haven: Yale University Press.

Goodenough, F. L. (1926). *Measurement of intelligence by drawings*. New York: Harcourt, Brace World.

Gresham, F. M. (1993). "What's wrong in this picture?": Response to Motta et al.'s review of Human figure drawings. *School Psychology, 8,* 182–186.

Gustafson, J. L., & Waehler, C. A. (1992). Assessing concrete and abstract thinking with the Draw-A-Person technique. *Journal of Personality Assessment, 59,* 439–447.

Hammer, E. (1958). *The clinical application of projective drawings*. Springfield, IL: Charles C. Thomas.

Harris, D. B. (1963). *Children's drawings as measures of intellectual activity*. New York: Harcourt Brace Jovanovich.

Hayslip, B., Cooper, C. C., Dougherty, L. M. & Cook, D. B. (1997). Body image in adulthood: A projective approach. *Journal of Personality Assessment, 68,* 628–649.

Houston, A. N., & Terwilliger, R. (1995). Sex, sex roles, and sexual attitudes: Figure gender in the Draw-A-Person test revisited. *Journal of Personality Assessment, 65,* 343–357.

Joiner, T. E., & Schmidt, K. L. (1997). Drawing conclusions- or not - from drawings. *Journal of Personality Assessment, 69,* 476–481.

Joiner, T. E., Schmidt, K. L., & Barnett, J. (1996). Size, detail, and line heaviness in children's drawings as correlates of emotional distress: (More) negative evidence. *Journal of Personality Assessment, 67,* 127–141.

Jolles, I. (1971). *A catalog for the qualitative interpretation of the House-Tree-Person (H-T-P), revised.* Los Angeles: Western Psychological Services.

Kahill, S. (1984). Human figure drawings in adults: An update of the empirical evidence, 1967–1982. *Canadian Psychology, 25,* 269–292.

Kamphaus, R. W., & Pleiss, K. L. (1993). Comment on "The use and abuse of human figure drawings." *School Psychology, 8,* 191–196.

Klepsch, M., & Logie, L. (1982). *Children draw and tell: An introduction to the projective uses of children's human figure drawings.* New York: Brunner/Mazel.

Klopfer, W. G., & Taulbee, E. S. (1976). Projective tests. *Annual Review of Psychology, 27,* 543–567.

Knoff, H. M. (1993). The utility of human figure drawings in personality and intellectual assessment: Why ask why? *School Psychology, 8,* 191–196.

Kohut, H. (1971). *The analysis of the self.* New York: International Universities Press.

Kohut, H. (1977). *The restoration of the self.* New York: International Universities Press.

Kohut, H. (1984). *How does analysis cure?* A. Goldberg & P. Stepansky (Eds.). Chicago: University of Chicago Press.

Koppitz, E. M. (1968). *Psychological evaluation of human figure drawings.* New York: Grune & Stratton.

Koppitz, E. M. (1984). *Psychological evaluation of human figure drawings by middle school pupils.* New York: Grune & Stratton.

Kot, J., Handler, L., Toman, K., & Hilsenroth, M. (1994). *A psychological assessment of homeless men.* Paper presented at the annual meeting of the Society of Personality Assessment, Chicago.

Lee, R. R., & Martin, J. C. (1991). *Psychotherapy after Kohut: A textbook of self psychology.* Hillsdale, NJ: The Analytic Press.

Lichtenberg, J. D. (1989). *Psychoanalysis and motivation.* Hillsdale, NJ: The Analytic Press.

Lichtenberg, J. D., Lachmann, F. M., & Fosshage, J. L. (1992). *Self and motivational systems: Toward a theory of psychological technique.* Hillsdale, NJ: The Analytic Press.

Luscher, M. (1969). The Luscher Color Test. I. Scott (Ed.). New York: Washington Square Press.

Machover, K. (1949). *Personality projection in the drawing of the human figure.* Springfield, IL: Charles C. Thomas.

Marsh, D. T., Linberg, L. M., & Smeltzer, J. K. (1991). Human figure drawings of adjudicated and nonadjudicated adolescents. *Journal of Personality Assessment, 57,* 77–86.

Mitchell, J., Trent, R., & McArthur, R. (1993). *Human Figure Drawing Test (HDFT).* Los Angeles: Western Psychological Services.

Motta, R. W., Little, S. G., & Tobin, M. I. (1993). The use and abuse of human figure drawings. *School Psychology, 8,* 162–169.

Naglieri, J. A. (1988). *Draw-A-Person: Quantitative scoring system.* San Antonio, TX: The Psychological Corporation.

Naglieri, J. A., McNeish, T. J., & Bardos, A. N. (1991). *Draw-A-Person: Screening procedure for emotional disturbance.* Austin, TX: Pro-Ed.

Oas, P. (1985). Clinical utility of an index on impulsivity on the Draw-A-Person test. *Perceptual and Motor Skills, 60,* 310.

Ogdon, D. P. (1967). *Psychodagnostics and personality assessment: A handbook.* (2nd ed.). Los Angeles: Western Psychological Services.

Ogdon, D. P. (1981). *Handbook of psychological signs, symptoms, and syndromes.* Los Angeles: Western Psychological Services.

Oster, G. D., & Gould, P. (1987). *Using drawings in assessment and therapy: A guide for mental health professionals.* New York: Brunner/Mazel.

Riethmiller, R. J., & Handler, L. (1997a). Problematic methods and unwarranted conclusions in DAP research: Suggestions for improved research procedures. *Journal of Personality Assessment, 69,* 459–475.

Riethmiller, R. J., & Handler, L. (1997b). The great figure drawing controversy: The integration of research and clinical practice. *Journal of Personality Assessment, 69,* 488–496.

Reznikoff, M., & Reznikoff, H. R. (1956). The family drawing test: A comparative study of children's drawings. *Journal of Clinical Psychology, 20,* 467–470.

Robins, C. E., Blatt, S. J., & Ford, R. Q. (1991). Changes in Human Figure Drawings during intensive treatment. *Journal of Personality Assessment, 57,* 477–497.

Rowe, C. E., & MacIsaac, D. S. (1989). *Empathic attunement: The technique of psychoanalytic self psychology.* Northvale, NJ: Jason Aronson.

Sims, J., Dana, R., & Bolton, B. (1983). Validity of the Draw-A-Person Test as an anxiety measure. *Journal of Abnormal Psychology, 47,* 250–256.

Sola, S. & Snyder, J. (1996). *A self psychological approach to assessment.* Paper presented at the International Congress of Rorschach, Boston.

Stolorow, R. D., Brandschaft, B., & Atwood, G. E. (1987). *Psychoanalytic treatment: An intersubjective approach.* Hillsdale, NJ: The Analytic Press.

Stolorow, R. D., Atwood, G. E., & Brandschaft, B. (1994). *The intersubjective perspective.* Northvale, NJ: The Analytic Press.

Suinn, R. M., & Oskamp, S. (1969). *The predictive validity of projective measures: A fifteen year evaluative review of research.* Springfield, IL: Charles C. Thomas.

Swensen, C. H. (1957). Empirical evaluation of human figure drawings. *Psychological Bulletin, 54,* 431–466.

Swensen, C. H. (1968). Empirical evaluation of human figure drawings: 1957–1966. *Psychological Bulletin, 70,* 20–44.

Tharanger, D. J., & Stark, K. (1990). A qualitative versus quantitative approach to evaluating the Draw-A-Person and Kinetic Family Drawings: A study of mood- and anxiety-disordered children. *Psychological Assessment, 2,* 365–375.

Urban, W. H. (1963). *The Draw-A-Person catalogue for interpretive analysis.* Los Angeles: Western Psychological Services.

Waldman, T. L., Silber, D. E., Holmstrom, R. W., & Karp, S. A. (1994). Personality characteristics of incest survivors on the Draw-A-Person Questionnaire. *Journal of Personality Assessment, 63,* 97–104.

Wenck, L. S. (1977). *House-Tree-Person drawings: An illustrated diagnostic handbook.* Los Angeles: Western Psychological Services.

Witkin, H. A., Dyk, R. B., Faterson, H. F., Goodenough, D. R., & Karp, S. A. (1962). *Psychological differentiation.* New York: Wiley.

Wolf, E. (1988). *Treating the self.* New York: Guilford.

Yama, M. F. (1990). The usefulness of human figure drawings as an index of overall adjustment. *Journal of Personality Assessment, 54,* 78–86.

INDEX